Bridges

Ponts

Brücken

Coordination and texts • *Coordination et rédaction* • Koordination und Redaktion
Martha Torres Arcila

Editorial Manager • *Direction éditoriale* • Verlagdirektor
Nacho Asensio

Design and layout • *Design graphique et maquette* • Design und Grafik
Carlos Gamboa Permanyer

Translation • *Traduction* • Übersetzung
Serena Chiang (english)
Anne Ouvrard (français)
Betty Springer (deutsch)

Production • *Production* • Produktion
Juanjo Rodríguez Novel

038669

03/03 HARVARD Books # 36.32

Copyright © 2002 Atrium Group
Editorial project::
  Books Factory, S.L.
e-mail: books@booksfactory.org

Published by: Atrium Internacional
de México, S.A. de C.V.
Fresas n° 60 (Colonia del Valle)
03200 México D.F. MÉXICO

Tel: +525 575 90 94
Fax: +525 559 21 52
e-mail: atriumex@prodigy.net.mx
www.atriumbooks.com

ISBN: 84-95692-61-9
Legal Deposit: B-36450-2002

Printed in Spain
Grabasa, S.L.

Copyright © 2002 Atrium Group
Projet éditorial :
  Books Factory, S.L.
e-mail: books@booksfactory.org

Publié par : Atrium Internacional de
México, S.A. de C.V.
Fresas n° 60 (Colonia del Valle)
03200 México D.F. MÉXICO

Tél: +525 575 90 94
Fax: +525 559 21 52
e-mail: atriumex@prodigy.net.mx
www.atriumbooks.com

ISBN: 84-95692-61-9
Dépôt légal : B-36450-2002

Imprimé en Espagne
Grabasa, S.L.

Copyright © 2002 Atrium Group
Verlag:
  Books Factory, S.L.
e-mail: books@booksfactory.org

Veröffentlicht durch: Atrium
Internacional de México, SA de C.V.
Fresas n° 60 (Colonia del Valle)
03200 México D.F. MÉXICO

Tel: +525 575 90 94
Fax: +525 559 21 52
e-mail: atriumex@prodigy.net.mx
www.atriumbooks.com

ISBN: 84-95692-61-9
Hinterlegung der Pflichtexemplare:
B-36450-2002

Gedruckt in Spanien
Grabasa, S.L.

Bridges

Ponts

Brücken

INDEX · SOMMAIRE · INH

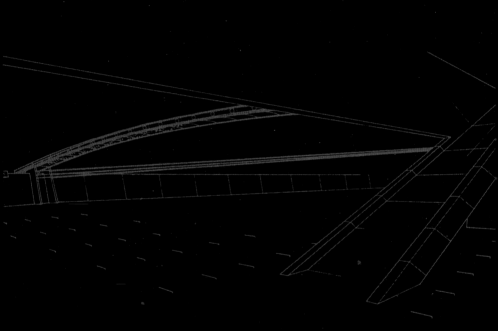

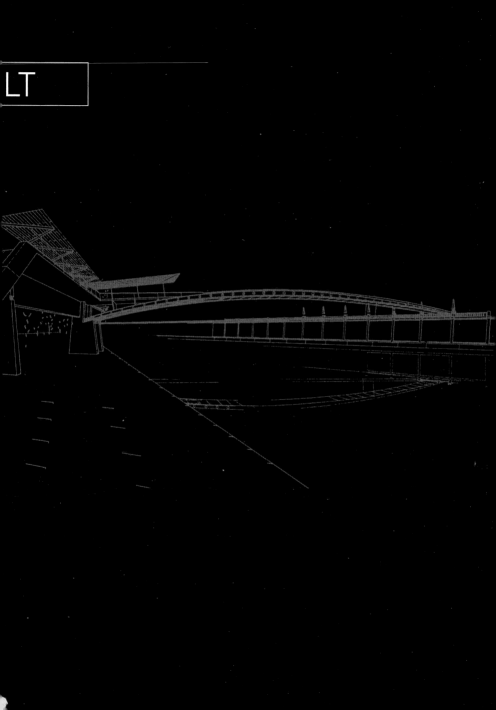

INTRODUCTION

Since the beginning of time, the need to overcome obstacles in order to provide continuity to a route has spurred the study of different methods for dealing with this issue. Thus, as humankind evolved, the first elements for surmounting these natural and artificial barriers emerged. However, as a result of these attempts to extend roadways, more complex needs became evident, for example, the need to expand cities which had become isolated behind mountains, or the need for communication between different regions in order to facilitate interchange. The structures which we refer to today as bridges were born as a result of this fact and thanks to technological advances. In this monograph we hope to present a general view of this subject by means of a variety of examples of these structures – whether already in existence or still in project – which provide passage over natural and artificial obstacles. With this idea, we will discover a wide diversity of projects: classified either according to their structural typology (suspension bridges, cable-stayed bridges, arch bridges, drawbridges) or according to the obstacle which they overcome (viaducts, elevated highways, overpasses).

We have nonetheless included not only the great bridges which involve numerous engineering techniques offering innovative structural solutions, but also projects of an exclusively pedestrian nature, for example footbridges, which constitute an important part of the subject of this book, albeit to a lesser extent. Hence, we will find a broad spectrum of projects, including not only those which offer innovative construction systems, designs or materials, but also those which have taken special care of the traditional elements in order to create an exceptionally fine aesthetic quality.

Regarding the use of this book, the projects included herein are presented in chronological order, thus providing the reader with an immediate view of the technological and aesthetic progress in this field. Nonetheless, it is not to present this subject from a historical point of view, as we have intentionally introduced only those projects which date from the 1950's onwards.

Each bridge and footbridge has been organized as a chapter unto itself including photographs and architectural plans preceded by a short introduction and the list of technical credits. With reference to the section on dates, the first date is the year of design and the second that of the finished work. However, when these two dates are separated by a slash, we are referring to bridges which have been expanded or otherwise subjected to subsequent interventions.

Hence, the information presented in each chapter is intended to transmit, at a glance, the essential facts about each bridge as well as its most important features.

Finally, we must add that some of the projects which we would have liked to include were nonetheless omitted from this selection due to the impossibility of recovering the required material from the firms in some cases, and in others to the fact that the material recovered was technically unfit for publication.

In spite of this, we feel that the final result of this monograph is a presentation which permits a global approach to the subject on hand. A subject which we believe to be of great importance due to the fact that, thanks to the progress achieved in this field, countries which promote the construction of bridges have attained enormous development in their economic, cultural and tourist activities, consequences that – like the bridges themselves – transcend also the political barriers.

MARTHA TORRES ARCILA

INTRODUCTION

En réponse au besoin de franchir les obstacles pour pouvoir aller plus loin, l'homme étudie depuis des siècles différents systèmes pour y parvenir. Ainsi, avec le développement de l'espèce humaine sont nés les premiers éléments permettant de surmonter frontières naturelles ou artificielles. Mais leur naissance a également engendré des besoins plus complexes pour pouvoir prolonger ces routes: l'expansion de villes jusqu'alors isolées par une colline, ou encore la liaison entre différents villages pour faciliter les échanges. En conséquence, et grâce aux progrès de la technologie, les structures que l'on connaît aujourd'hui sous le nom de ponts sont apparues. Cette monographie vise à donner une vue d'ensemble de cette thématique en s'appuyant sur des exemples de structures, construites ou non, servant à surmonter obstacles naturels ou artificiels.

Sont compris dans cet ouvrage non seulement les grands ponts où les techniques d'ingénierie employées ont permis des solutions structurelles novatrices, mais également des projets exclusivement piétons comme les passerelles, qui, bien qu'à plus petite échelle, constituent une partie importante de la thématique proposée ici. Vous découvrirez un large éventail de projets: certains innovateurs par leur système de construction, leur conception ou le matériel utilisé, d'autres regroupant avec soin tous les éléments traditionnels pour parvenir à une qualité esthétique exceptionnelle.

Les projets qui figurent dans le présent ouvrage sont présentés par ordre chronologique, ce qui offre au lecteur une vision immédiate des progrès technologiques et esthétiques ayant eu lieu dans ce domaine. Il ne faut cependant pas considérer cela comme une vision historique: nous avons intentionnellement favorisé des projets remontant seulement au milieu du vingtième siècle, voire plus tard.

Chaque pont ou passerelle prend la forme d'un chapitre, accompagné de photos et de plans architecturaux précédés d'une brève introduction et d'une fiche technique. En ce qui concerne les dates qui apparaissent, il faut signaler que la première correspond à la date du projet, et la seconde situe l'année où l'œuvre a été achevée. Quand une barre oblique les sépare, cela signifie que le pont a subi ultérieurement agrandissement ou modifications.

Par conséquent, le contenu de chaque chapitre est présenté de telle sorte qu'une première lecture du projet suffit à connaître les données basiques et les éléments d'importance.

En dernier lieu, il convient de noter que certains des projets que nous souhaitions inclure dans cet ouvrage n'y figurent pas, et ce, soit parce qu'il fut impossible à plusieurs reprises de récupérer le matériel des archives, soit parce que ce matériel n'était pas techniquement valable pour une publication.

Nous estimons toutefois que le résultat final de cette monographie permet une approche globale du thème abordé, thème que nous considérons d'une grande importance. Les progrès dans ce domaine ont permis le développement de pays où la construction de ponts est promue, engendrant dès lors des bénéfices reflétés dans leurs activités économiques, culturelles et touristiques, conséquences qui, de même que les ponts, permettent de franchir les frontières politiques.

MARTHA TORRES ARCILA

EINLEITUNG

Das Bedürfnis des Menschen Hindernisse zu überwinden um seinen Weg fortsetzen zu können, hat ihn schon in Urzeiten zu der Suche nach Systemen zur Überquerung veranlasst. Schon in Frühstadien der Entwicklung der Menschheit gab es Ideen und erste Elemente,die es ermöglichten, natürliche und künstliche Grenzen zu bezwingen. Gleichzeitig aber warfen diese ersten Versuche neue, komplexere Notwendigkeiten der Wegfortsetzung auf, wie zum Beispiel die Ausdehnung von Städten, die durch einen Hügel isoliert sind, oder die Verbindung von Dörfern um deren Kommunikation untereinander zu ermöglichen. Dank der frühen Anstrengungen und des Fortschritts der Technologie, wurden bereits vor langer Zeit die Strukturen geboren, die wir heute als Brücken kennen. Das Ziel dieses monografisch angelegten Buches ist es, mit Hilfe von Beispielen verschiedener Strukturen zur Überwindung von natürlichen oder künstlichen Hindernissen —von denen sich einige noch im Bau befinden—, einen allgemeinen Überblick zu dieser Thematik zu geben. Wir werden diversen Projekte begegnen, die sich in ihrer Bauweise (Hängebrücken, Schrägseilbrücken, Bogenbrücken, Klappbrücken) oder in der Art des zu bezwingenden Hindernisses (Viadukte, Hochstraßen, Überführungen) unterscheiden.

Allerdings haben wir nicht nur die großen Brücken, an deren Bau unzählige Ingenieure mit Ideen für neue strukturelle Lösungen beteiligt waren, bedacht sondern schenken unsere Aufmerksamkeit auch kleineren Überführungen, die zum Beispiel nur für Fußgänger gedacht sind. Also werden wir eine Auswahl der unterschiedlichsten Projekte kennenlernen: die innovativen bezüglich ihrer Konstruktionssysteme und Baumaterialien und auch die klassischen und traditionellen, die ganz besonderen Wert auf die ästhetische Qualität ihres Ergebnisses legten. Die

Reihenfolge der in diesem Buch betrachteten Brücken ist chronologisch, was dem Leser einen sofortigen Überblick über die technologischen und ästhetischen Fortschritte jeder einzelnen Epoche verschafft. Trotzdem kann diese Sammlung nicht als ein historischer Abriss betrachtet werden, da wir uns nur auf die Bauwerke ab der fünfziger Jahre des 20. Jahrhunderts aufwärts konzentriert haben.

Jeder Brücke ist ein eigenes kurzes Kapitel mit Fotos, Skizzen, einer Einleitung und den jeweiligen technischen Angaben gewidmet. Zur Datumsangabe ist zu erwähnen, dass sich das zuerst angegebene Jahr auf die Entstehung des Projekts und das zweite auf die Fertigstellung der Bauarbeiten bezieht. Sind die Jahreszahlen durch Schrägstriche getrennt, weist das darauf hin, dass die Brücke nach ihrer Einweihung Gegenstand einer Erweiterung oder anderweitigen Veränderung war.Das in jedem Kapitel präsentierte Material hat es zum Zweck, den Leser über die Grunddaten eines jeden Projekts und seine Besonderheiten und Auffälligkeiten zu informieren.

Am Ende ist noch zu erwähnen, dass wir einige wichtige Brücken nicht in diese Sammlung aufnehmen konnten, da es uns unmöglich war Informationen zu bestimmten Projekten zu erhalten oder diese nur unvollständig und somit nicht zur Veröffentlichung geeignet waren.

Trotzdem wird Ihnen dieses Buch einen Gesamtüberblick über ein wichtiges und interessantes Thema verschaffen —die Brücken unserer Erde. Brücken, die der wirtschaftlichen Entwicklung vieler Länder entscheidende Impulse gegeben haben und deren Nutzen sich nicht nur im ökonomischen Bereich sondern auch in einem kulturellen und touristischen Zusammenhang widerspiegelt. Der Einfluss und Effekt der bedeutendsten Brücken ist international spürbar und grenzüberschreitend— genau wie viele der Bauwerke selbst.

MARTHA TORRES ARCILA

Williamsburg Bridge

Llefert L. Buck, ing. 1903
Parsons. 1999-2005

NEW YORK, USA. 1903 / 1999-2005

Length / Longueur / Gesamtlänge 2229 m.
Span / Travée / Hauptspannweite 487 m.

This bridge, inaugurated in 1903, with traces reminiscent of the aesthetic style of the engineer Gustave Eiffel, was constructed for the purpose of joining Brooklyn and Manhattan. Its typology is that of the suspension bridge with a metallic structure. With the passing of the years and as a result of various inspections, the New York State Department of Transportation undertook a rehabilitation project in the 1990's. Through the design of an innovative deck rehabilitation system, this project, with deadline planned for the year 2005, is being carried out with a strict adherence to the schedule. Every effort is being made to interfere with the normal functioning of the bridge as little as possible.

Rappelant l'esthétique de l'ingénieur Gustave Eiffel, ce pont, inauguré en 1903, a été construit dans le but de relier Brooklyn à Manhattan. C'est un pont de type suspendu, de structure métallique. Au fil des ans et suite à divers contrôles, le Service des Transports de New York entreprend dans les années 90 un programme de restauration. Grâce à l'utilisation d'un tout nouveau système pour la restauration de la plateforme, le projet respecte strictement les délais fixés pour sa réalisation, prévue pour 2005, pratiquement sans interférer avec le bon fonctionnement du pont.

Diese Hängebrücke mit metallischer Grundstruktur, die eindeutige Spuren des Stils des Ingenieurs Gustav Eiffel aufweist, wurde im Jahre 1903 fertiggestellt und verbindet die Stadtteile Brooklyn und Manhattan. Nach mehreren Inspektionen hat das New Yorker Transportbüro in den neunziger Jahren ein Rehabilitationsprojekt für die Brücke in die Wege geleitet. Die Modernisierung der Plattform wird mit Hilfe eines neuen Systems durchgeführt, das die gewohnte Bewegung auf der Williamsburg Bridge kaum beeinträchtigt. Der vereinbarte Zeitplan wird strikt eingehalten, wodurch die Restaurierung voraussichtlich im Jahr 2005 beendet sein wird.

In spite of its age and thanks to the excellent maintenance service, the Williamsburg Bridge continues to be one of the most heavily used bridges in New York. It boasts a total of 8 lanes and remains, even today, one of the longest suspension bridges in the world.

Malgré son grand âge, et grâce à un entretien régulier, Williamsburg Bridge, avec 8 voies de dépassement, est aujourd'hui encore l'un des ponts les plus fréquentés de New York, et l'un des ponts suspendus les plus grands du monde entier.

Trotz ihres Alters und dank eines effektiven Instandhaltungssystems ist die Williamsburg Bridge mit ihren acht Fahrspuren noch immer eine der meist benutzten Brücken New Yorks und eine der längsten Hängebrücken der Welt.

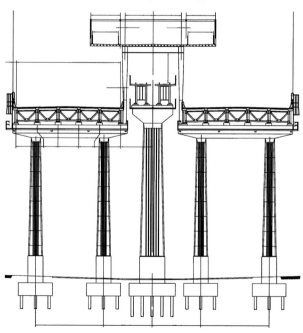

Carquinez Strait Bridges

D.B Steinman. 1927, 1958
Parsons; OPAC. 2000-2005

VALLEJO, CROCKETT (CALIFORNIA), USA. 1927 / 1958 / 2000-2005

Length / Longueur / Gesamtlänge 1059 m.
Span / Travée / Hauptspannweite 728 m.

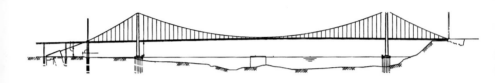

Two bridges with a metallic structure were built over the Strait of Carquinez in 1927 and 1958. These constituted the point of union with the city of San Francisco. When their expansion became an almost ineludible necessity, an analysis of the existing structures demonstrated their obvious deterioration. The result was the construction of a new bridge which in the future would replace the old passages. After studying different proposals, which included ideas such as "copying" the bridges already in existence, to the solution of using arches in the main structure, the decision was made to select a visually lighter model such as the suspension bridge.

Entre en 1927 et 1958, deux ponts de structure métallique sont construit sur le détroit de Carquinez, et constituent un point d'attache avec la ville de San Francisco. Quand leur élargissement devient impératif, l'analyse des structures existantes révèle leur détérioration, ce qui aboutit au projet de construction d'un nouveau pont pour remplacer les anciens passages. A partir de l'étude de différentes propositions, qui vont des «copies» de ponts existants à la solution de l'arc comme structure principale, le choix se porte finalement sur un modèle plus léger visuellement comme l'est le pont suspendu.

Úber die Meerenge von Carquinez wurden in den Jahren 1927 und 1958 zwei Brücken metallischer Struktur gebaut, die einen Verbindungspunkt mit der Stadt San Francisco darstellten. Als deren Erweiterung unvermeidlich und im Zuge der Planungen die Struktur der Bauten gründlich analysiert wurde, kam der bereits sehr schlechte Zustand der Brücken zum Vorschein. Somit wurde der Bau einer neuen Brücke geplant, die die alten Zufahrtswege ersetzen sollte. Nachdem verschiedene Entwürfe studiert wurden und die Vorschläge einer "Kopie" der alten Brücken und auch die Idee einer Bogenbrücke verworfen wurden, entschied man sich für die optisch leichtere Struktur einer Hängebrücke.

SUPERSTRUCTURE SECTION

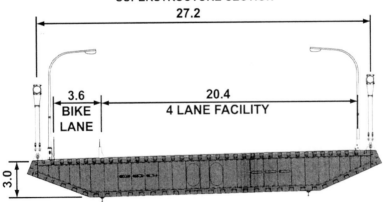

27.2

3.6
BIKE
LANE

20.4
4 LANE FACILITY

3.0

- STEEL ORTHOTROPIC BOX
- WELDED FIELD SPLICES ASSUMED
- OPTIONAL BOLTED FIELD SPLICES OK EXCEPT TOP PLATE

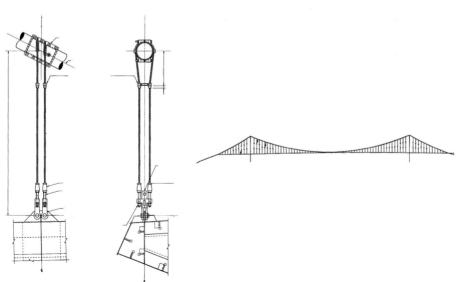

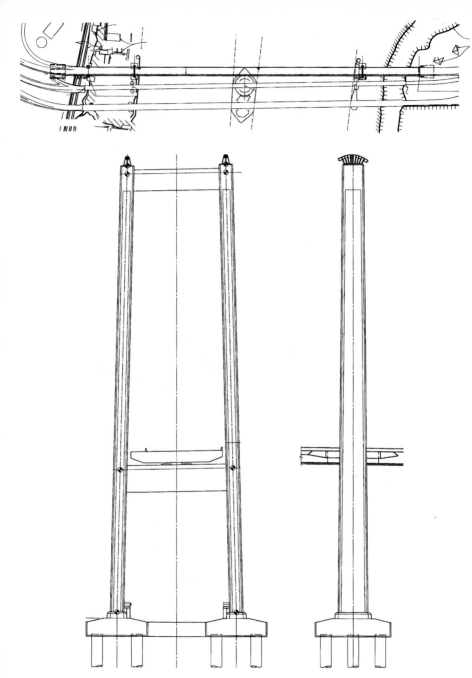

The Strait of Carquinez, which carries the Sacramento River to San Francisco Bay, is the site of this project. These aging metal structures will be completely replaced by the new suspension bridge.

La scène du projet est le détroit de Carquinez, qui relie la rivière Sacramento à la Baie de San Francisco. Les anciennes structures métalliques seront toutes remplacées par un nouveau pont suspendu.

Die Meerenge von Carquinez, die den Sacramento zur Bucht von San Francisco führt, ist der Schauplatz dieses Projekts. Die alten Metallstrukturen werden bald vollständig durch eine Hängebrücke ersetzt sein.

Lions Gate Bridge

First Narrows Bridge Company. 1937-1938
Steinman Boynton Gronquist & Birdsall
Buckland & Taylor, Ltd. 1975

VANCOUVER-BC, CANADA. 1937-1938 / 1975

Length / Longueur / Gesamtlänge 1600 m.
Span / Travée / Hauptspannweite 472 m.

The first initiative for the construction of this bridge had already been proposed by the end of the 19th century. After a lengthy process overcoming a variety of obstacles, construction finally began in 1937. This bridge, located in an attractive natural scenic area, is one of the entryways to the port of Vancouver, the Canadian gateway to the Pacific. The chosen structural design is that of the suspension bridge with a narrow deck, which has been subjected throughout the years to different maintenance and restoration interventions. The most important of these occurred in 1975, when the original deck was replaced by a metal one which increased the original width.

Les premières tentatives pour construire ce pont remontent à la fin du 19ème siècle. Après un long processus et divers obstacles à surmonter, sa construction peut enfin commencer en 1937. Situé dans un site naturel attrayant, ce pont constitue l'une des entrées du port de Vancouver, un port canadien qui s'ouvre sur le Pacifique. La structure choisie est celle du pont suspendu, avec une plate-forme étroite ayant subi avec le temps diverses interventions de maintenance et de restauration, dont la plus importante date de 1975, quand une plate-forme métallique plus large remplace l'originale.

Die ersten Initiativen zum Bau dieser Brücke führen bis zum Ende des 19. Jahrhunderts zurück. Wegen vieler unerwartet auftretender Schwierigkeiten und langen Beratungen und Berechnungen wurde ihr Bau aber erst im Jahr 1937 begonnen. Vor der Kulisse einer besonders attraktiven Landschaft stellt diese Brücke einen der Zugänge zum Hafen von Vancouver und gleichzeitig das kanadische Tor zum Pazifischen Ozean dar. Das gewählte strukturelle Schema der Brücke ist das einer Hänge-brücke mit schmaler Plattform. Im Laufe der Jahre wurde der Bau mehreren Restaurierungen und Instandhaltungsarbeiten unterzogen, wobei die wichtigste 1975 durchgeführt wurde, als seine Plattform durch eine etwas breitere, metallische ersetzt wurde.

The chosen structural design is that of the suspension bridge with a narrow deck, which has been subjected throughout the years to different maintenance and restoration interventions.

La structure choisie est celle du pont suspendu, avec une plate-forme étroite qui a subi avec le temps diverses interventions d'entretien et de restauration.

Das gewählte strukturelle Schema dieses Brückenbaus ist das einer Hängebrücke mit schmaler Plattform, welche im Laufe der Jahre schon einigen Restaurierungen und Instandhaltungsarbeiten unterzogen wurde.

The Lions Gate Bridge has a unique character: because of its history, location and importance as a connecting piece it is one of the oldest bridges in the area which remains in use today, thanks largely to the interventions of its maintenance service.

Son histoire, son emplacement et son importance en tant que moyen de connexion font du Lions Gate Bridge une composition unique, figurant parmi les plus anciennes de cette région toujours en service, dû en grande partie aux opérations de maintenance.

Die Lions Gate Bridge hat einen einmaligen Charakter: durch seine Geschichte, Lage und Bedeutung ist es eine der ältesten sich noch im Gebrauch befindlichen Brücken dieser Gegend, was hauptsächlich den regelmäßigen Bemühungen um ihre Instandhaltung zu verdanken ist.

Tacoma & New Tacoma Narrows Bridge

Leon Moseff, Clark Eldridge. 1940
United Infrastructure; Parsons. 2000
Pierce County (Washington), USA. 1940-1950 / 2000-2005

Length / Longueur / Gesamtlänge 1671 m.
Span / Travée / Hauptspannweite 864 m.

Since 1928, studies were made concerning the possibility of connecting Tacoma with the Port of Gig. Actual construction, however, of the Tacoma Narrows Bridge – also known as Galloping Gertie – did not begin until 1940. This slender and airy suspension bridge, revolutionary for its times, nevertheless collapsed a few months after its inauguration. In 1950 a new and safer bridge was inaugurated. Due to the increase in traffic along the SR16 highway, however, this new bridge needed to be widened with an additional structure. Thus we find the New Tacoma Narrows Bridge alongside the old one, with modern technology but the same formal design as the preceding bridges.

On étudiait depuis 1928 un moyen de relier Tacoma et le port de Gig, mais il a fallu attendre 1940 avant que le Tacoma Narrows Bridge – également connu sous le nom de Galloping Gertie – se construise. Malgré tout, ce pont léger et tout en longueur, révolutionnaire pour l'époque, s'effondre quelques mois après son inauguration. Un nouveau pont, plus solide, est inauguré en 1950, et doit être agrandi au moyen d'une structure complémentaire, dû à l'augmentation de circulation sur la voie rapide SR16. Ainsi, le New Tacoma Narrows Bridge est construit à côté de l'ancien, à partir de technologies plus modernes mais en conservant le même schéma.

Bereits seit 1928 wurde die Verbindung zwischen Tacoma und dem Hafen von Gig studiert, aber erst 1940 kam es tatsächlich zum Bau der Tacoma Narrows Bridge, die auch unter dem Namen Galloping Gertie bekannt ist. Diese leichte und elegante Hängebrücke, die für ihre Zeit revolutionär war, brach allerdings nur wenige Monate nach ihrer Einweihung zusammen. Im Jahre 1950 wurde der Bau einer neuen sichereren Brücke fertiggestellt, die später durch die starke Verdichtung des Verkehrs auf der Schnellstraße SR16 mit einem zusätzlichen Bau erweitert werden musste. Heutzutage ist also neben der alten die New Tacoma Narrows Bridge zu sehen, die zwar unter Anwendung moderner Technologien gebaut aber optisch dem Schema der älteren Brücke nachempfunden wurde.

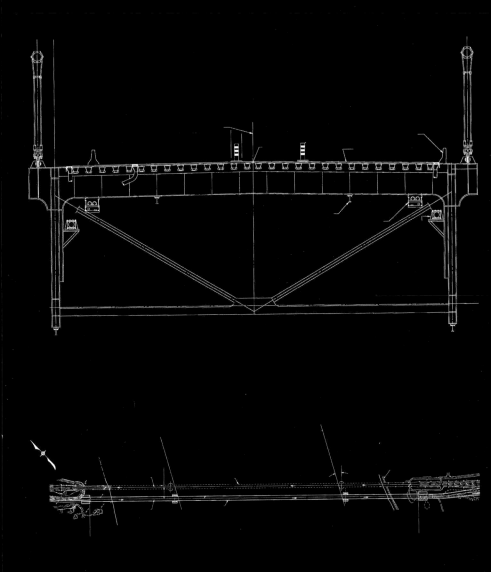

The construction of a bridge between Tacoma and the Port of Gig had been studied since the 1920's; although the first bridge only came into existence in 1940, it was not until 1950 when the connection truly became a reality.

Depuis les années 20 du siècle passé, des études avaient été menées sur la construction d'un pont entre Tacoma et le port de Gig. Même si un pont existait déjà en 1940, la connexion ne s'établit réellement que dix années plus tard.

Seit den zwanziger Jahren des vergangenen Jahrhunderts war der Bau einer Brücke zwischen Tacoma und dem Hafen von Gig bereits im Gespräch, aber erst 1950 kam eine permanente Verbindung zustande.

Woodrow Wilson Bridge

HNTB, ing. 1961
Parsons. 2000-2004

PRINCE GEORGE'S COUNTY (MARYLAND), USA. 1961 / 2000-2004

Length / Longueur / Gesamtlänge 1852 m.
Span / Travée / Hauptspannweite 124 m.

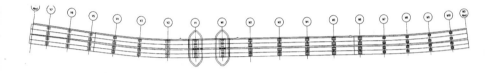

This is an example of an old bridge in need of expansion due to its proximity to a large city. In 1961 the Woodrow Wilson Bridge was inaugurated as a passageway over the Potomac River, but as the years went by the flow of traffic over this river suffered a steady increase. For this reason a second Woodrow Wilson Bridge must soon be planned. As a part of the monumental area of the Metropolitan Region of Washington, the whiteness of its structure reminds us of the colour of the marble used in the great commemorative monuments of the region. Its typology is based on the arch which supports a continuous deck which would permit the construction of new lanes over the river.

Ceci est un exemple de pont ancien qui, étant situé près d'une grande ville, doit s'agrandir. Le Woodrow Wilson Bridge est inauguré en 1961 comme moyen de passage sur la rivière Potomac, mais avec l'afflux de voitures, il s'agrandit peu à peu, jusqu'au moment où il devient nécessaire de créer un deuxième Woodrow Wilson Bridge. A l'intérieur de la zone monumentale de l'arrondissement urbain de Washington, le blanc de sa structure rappelle la couleur du marbre des grands monuments commémoratifs existants dans la région. Sa typologie est celle de l'arc qui supporte une plate-forme continue, permettant la construction de nouveaux canaux sur la rivière.

Hier haben wir ein Beispiel einer alten Brücke, die durch ihre Nähe zu einer großen Stadt erweitert werden muss. Im Jahr 1961 wurde die Woodrow Wilson Bridge über dem Potomac eingeweiht, aber durch das ständige Ansteigen der Anzahl Autos, die den Fluss täglich überqueren, wird schon bald eine zweite Woodrow Wilson Bridge von Nöten sein. Als Teil der Denkmalzone des Stadtgebiets Washington ist die Farbgebung der Brücke der weißen Farbe des Marmors der großen Denkmäler, die in dieser Gegend häufig zu sehen sind, angepasst. Die Brücke besteht aus Bögen, die eine Plattform tragen und die Möglichkeit des Baus weiterer Fahrbahnen über dem Fluss offenlassen.

The first bridge was designed to support the weight of 75,000 vehicles per day. However, this figure has almost tripled in only 8 years, for which the inevitable deterioration of this bridge is imminent if the traffic flow is not controlled.

Le premier pont est prévu pour supporter une moyenne de 75000 véhicules par jour, chiffre qui triple en seulement 8 ans. Il faut alors contrôler l'afflux de voitures afin d'éviter la détérioration imminente du pont.

Die erste Brücke wurde für eine Belastung von 75.000 Fahrzeugen pro Tag berechnet und entworfen. Allerdings verdreifachte sich diese Ziffer in nur 8 Jahren, wodurch der Verschleiß der Brücke unaufhaltsam schnell voranschreiten würde, wäre der Zustrom nicht streng kontrolliert.

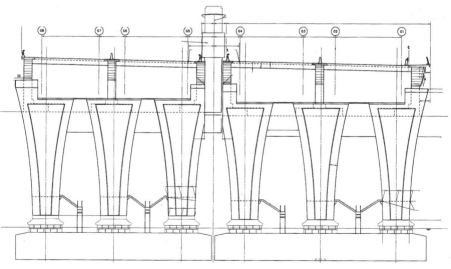

The four lanes crossing the Potomac River will be increased to 12 with the construction of the second Woodrow Wilson Bridge. In addition to car lanes, pedestrian and bicycle paths will also be included.

Il est prévu d'agrandir les quatre canaux de passage de la rivière Potomac pour en faire 12 canaux au total avec la construction du second Woodrow Wilson. En plus des voitures, piétons et bicyclettes pourront traverser.

Die Zahl der vier Fahrbahnen über dem Potomac werden bald mit dem Bau der zweiten Woodrow Wilson auf zwölf steigen. Außer der neuen Fahrspuren für Autos wird die neue Brücke auch über Fuß- und Radwege verfügen.

New Little Belt Bridge

Danish State Railways,
Monberg & Thorsen A/S

JUTLAND–FUNEN, DENMARK. 1965-1970

Length / Longueur / Gesamtlänge 1700 m.
Span / Travée / Hauptspannweite 600 m.

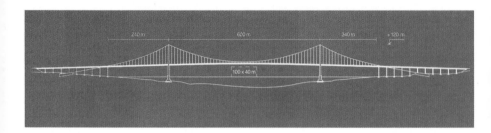

240 m   600 m   240 m   + 120 m

100 x 40 m

Because of its physical characteristics, the country of Denmark – composed of almost 400 islands which must be connected to the peninsula of Jutland (near northern Germany) – became an exemplary builder of a great number of bridges. Thanks to these bridges Denmark has optimized its commercial and economic relationships with Europe. In 1935 the first Little Belt Bridge was constructed with a deck for cars and trains. A new bridge was designed three decades later in order to join Jutland and Funen, bringing to six the number of lanes in use. With a total length of 1,700 m. and a span of 600 m., it is one of the longest bridges in Scandinavia.

*L**es caractéristiques géographiques du Danemark, composé de près de 400 îles qui doivent être reliées à la péninsule de Jutland, (vèrs le Nord de l'Allemagne), font de ce pays le «constructeur» de nombreux ponts, grâce auxquels le Danemark a pu optimiser ses relations commerciales et économiques avec l'Europe. Le premier pont Little Belt est construit en 1935, et dispose d'une plateforme pour les voitures et les trains. Une trentaine d'années plus tard, on projette l'élaboration d'un nouveau pont à 6 voies devant relier Jutland à Funen, de 1700 m de longueur et 600 m de travée, l'un des plus longs de la Scandinavie.*

Durch die physischen Eigenschaften des Landes Dänemark, das aus 400 Inseln besteht, die mit der Halbinsel Jütland im Norden Deutschlands verknüpft werden müssen, ist es schon seit langer Zeit ein besonders aktiver «Brückenbauer». Dank der großen Anzahl an Brücken hat Dänemark seine Wirtschaftsbeziehungen innerhalb Europas optimieren können. Im Jahr 1935 wurde die erste Little Belt Brücke gebaut, die Autos und Zügen die Überfahrt ermöglichte. Drei Jahrzehnte später baute man eine neue Brücke, die die Inseln Jütland und Funen verbindet. Sie verfügt über sechs Fahrspuren bei einer Gesamtlänge von 1700 m und einer Hauptspannweite von 600 m, was diese Brücke zu einer der längsten Skandinaviens macht.

The New Little Belt was one of Denmark's first suspension bridges. Its metal deck was built from pre-fabricated pieces which were later assembled during construction by crane barges.

New Little Belt est l'un des premiers ponts suspendus du Danemark. Sa plate-forme métallique est conçue à partir de pièces préfabriquées puis assemblées avec des bateaux-grues.

Die New Little Belt Bridge war eine der ersten Hängebrücken Dänemarks. Ihre metallische Plattform besteht aus vorgefertigten Teilen, die mit Schiffskränen montiert wurden.

Van Brienenoord Bridge

Rijkswaterstaat
W.Snieder, arq.
ROTTERDAM, HOLLAND. 1965,1989

Length / Longueur / Gesamtlänge 1300 m.

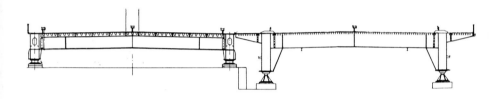

The Van Brienenoord Bridge was inaugurated in 1965 as part of the highway network in the vicinity of Rotterdam. With the passing of time it became necessary to plan an addition. For this reason a second passageway was built beside the first in 1989, increasing to 12 the number of lanes crossing the river and attaining thus the status of one of the four most important bridges across the Nieuwe Maas River. On account of the distance in time which separates the construction of the two bridges, we find ourselves before "one" single bridge combining two completely independent structures yet built one beside the other, complementing each other structurally and acting as one unique entity due to the minimum distance between them: a mere 15 cm.

Le pont Van Brienenoord a été inauguré en 1965; il fait partie du réseau routier proche de Rotterdam. Avec le temps, un agrandissement devient nécessaire; un second passage est construit à proximité en 1989, avec 12 canaux sur la rivière: c'est désormais l'un des quatre ponts les plus importants qui traversent la rivière Nieuwe Maas. A cause du laps de temps qui sépare les deux projets, nous nous trouvons face à «un» pont qui comprend deux structures indépendantes construites l'une à côté de l'autre, qui se complètent et agissent comme une seule et même structure, tant la distance qui les sépare est courte: 15 cm seulement.

Als Teil des Straßennetzes der nächsten Umgebung von Rotterdam wurde die Brücke Van Brienenoord 1965 eingeweiht. Eine Erweiterung des Baus wurde schon nach einigen Jahren unabdingbar und so baute man 1989 einen zweiten Überweg an seiner Seite und erweiterte die Anzahl der Fahrspuren auf zwölf, wodurch die Van Brienenoord zu einer der vier wichtigsten Brücken über den Fluss Nieuwe Maas wurde. Die Struktur, die wir heute sehein, scheint nur «eine» Brücke zu sein, die allerdings aus zwei unabhängigen besteht, die miteinander verbunden wurden. Der Abstand zwischen den beiden beträgt lediglich 15 cm.

46

During the construction of the second
structure and in spite of the exceptional
proximity between the two, the functioning of the original bridge was inter-
fered with as little as possible. It is for
this reason that this expansion project
stands out as exemplary.

*Pendant la construction de la deuxième
structure, et vu la proximité avec la première, il n'y a presque pas eu d'interfé-
rence avec le fonctionnement habituel
du pont d'origine, ce qui a permis un
projet d'agrandissement exemplaire.*

Während des Baus der zweiten Struktur
wurde, trotz der unmittelbaren Nähe zur
ersten Van Brienenoord, der Verkehr auf
dieser kaum beeinträchtigt, was die
Bauarbeiten zum Vorbild für andere
Erweiterungsprojekte machte.

Ponte 25 de Abril

American Bridge / Steinman Boynton Gronquist, London & New York. 1966
Steinman; Parsons; DSD Dillinger Stahlbau GmbH. 1999

LISBOA, PORTUGAL. 1966 / 1999

Length / Longueur / Gesamtlänge 3200 m.
Span / Travée / Hauptspannweite 1013 m.

This metallic suspension bridge, the winning design by two American companies in an international competition in 1966, broke several world records at its inauguration: it was the longest bridge in Europe with lanes for both cars and trains, it had the deepest pillars ever built until the date and its towers were the highest in the world. It is no wonder, then, that this work should become one of the icons of the city; for this reason, at the moment of planning an expansion, it was decided to build within the existing structure in order to affect its image as little as possible. As a result, the rehabilitation work and the expansion have done nothing less than strengthen the reputation of this bridge as a landmark.

Ce pont suspendu métallique conçu par deux sociétés américaines remporte en 1966 un concours international. Il bat plusieurs records lors de son inauguration: le pont le plus long d'Europe pouvant accueillir voitures et trains, les piliers les plus profonds jamais construits jusqu'à présent, et les tours les plus hautes. Il n'est donc pas surprenant que cette œuvre soit devenue l'un des symboles de la ville. Pour cette raison, le projet d'agrandissement prévoit de rester à l'intérieur même de la structure existante afin de nuire le moins possible à son image. Ainsi, la restauration et l'agrandissement de ce pont n'ont fait que renforcer son caractère.

Zwei amerikanische Firmen gewannen 1966 den Wettbewerb um den Bau dieser stählernen Hängebrücke und stellten seinerzeit einige Rekorde auf: es war die längste Brücke Europas für Autos und Züge, besaß die tiefsten je gebauten Pfeiler und auch die höchsten Türme. Die Brücke wurde zu einer der Ikonen der Stadt und als eine Erweiterung der Brücke notwendig wurde, beschloss man diese innerhalb der bereits bestehenden Struktur durchzuführen, um ihr Erscheinungsbild so wenig wie möglich zu verändern. Die Restaurierung und Erweiterung der Brücke haben ihren symbolischen Charakter noch weiter verstärkt.

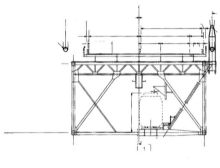

This proposal designed by the strategic union of two American companies won the competition for the construction of this metal-structured bridge, this perhaps is the origin of its subsequent formal connection to the Golden Gate Bridge of San Francisco (USA).

Le prix remporté par le projet de construction de ce pont de structure métallique, né de l'union stratégique de deux sociétés américaines, pourrait être à l'origine de ses connexions formelles avec le Golden Gate de San Francisco (USA).

Der Entwurf zweier kooperierender amerikanischer Firmen gewann den Wettbewerb zum Bau dieser Metallbrücke, was eine Erklärung für ihre Ähnlichkeit mit der Golden Gate Bridge in San Francisco in den USA sein könnte.

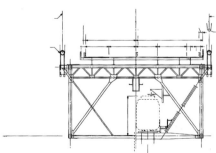

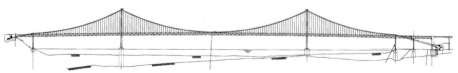

With the passing of the years this bridge over the Tagus River has become the undisputed landmark of the city: its imposing structure has been strengthened by the optimization of the functions intrinsic to a bridge.

Au fil des ans, le pont qui traverse le Tage est devenu le monument clé de la ville : sa structure imposante a pu être renforcée par l'optimisation des fonctions inhérentes à ce pont.

Im Laufe der Jahre hat sich diese Brücke über dem Tajo zweifelsohne zu dem Symbol Lissabons entwickelt; sie ist ein Beispiel für die optimale Verknüpfung einer imposanten Struktur mit der Funktionalität einer Brücke.

Bosporus Bridge

Freeman, Fox & Partners, ing.
Hochtief

ISTANBUL, TURKEY. 1970-1973

Length / Longueur / Gesamtlänge 1560 m.
Span / Travée / Hauptspannweite 1074 m.

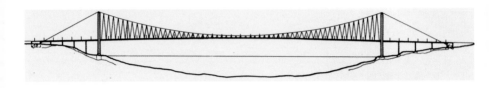

S ince distant times, the construction of a bridge over the Bosphorous River has been of great importance as it would constitute a strategic connection between Asia and southern Europe. It would in addition stimulate great development in the region. Nonetheless, the construction of this link between the Black Sea and the Sea of Marmara was not achieved until 1973. This connection would in turn come to form a part of the network of connections on a larger scale which reach from the Black to the Mediterranean Seas. This suspension bridge, still one of the largest of its typology today, is crossed daily by some 200 000 cars, a fact which confirms its enormous importace.

D *epuis des siècles, la réalisation d'un passage sur le Bosphore était primordiale, car cela constituait une connexion stratégique entre le sud de l'Europe et l'Asie, et signifiait également un important développement dans la région. Mais ce n'est qu'en 1973 que débute la construction d'une liaison entre la mer noire et la mer de Marmara, qui fera ensuite partie d'un réseau de connexions à plus grande échelle, reliant la mer noire à la méditerranée. Ce pont suspendu, aujourd'hui encore l'un des plus grands de sa catégorie, reçoit chaque jour quelques 200 000 voitures, ce qui vient confirmer sa grande importance.*

D er Bau einer Brücke über den Fluss Bosforo ist schon von jeher ein Projekt von großer Bedeutung gewesen, da dies eine Verbindung zwischen Südeuropa und Asien darstellt und einen wichtigen Impuls für die Entwicklung der Region mit sich bringt. Trotzdem hat es bis 1975 gedauert, bis ein Übergang zwischen dem Schwarzen Meer und dem Meer von Marmara geschaffen wurde, der gleichzeitig Teil des Verkehrsnetzes zwischen dem Schwarzen Meer und dem Mittelmeer ist. Die Hängebrücke, die noch immer zu einer der größten ihrer Art zählt, wird täglich von etwa 200 000 Autos überquert, was ihre große Bedeutung für den Verkehrsfluss bestätigt.

Humber River Bridge

Humber Bridge Board
Freeman Fox & Partners ing.

YORKSHIRE–LINCOLNSHIRE, UNITED KINGDOM. 1972-1981

Length / Longueur / Gesamtlänge 2220 m.
Span / Travée / Hauptspannweite 1410 m.

T owards the end of the 19th century the question was raised concerning the necessity of securing a connection between the two shores of this estuary. The first project, in fact, dates from the year 1872, when a tunnel was proposed. This project was nonetheless considered unviable due to the high cost of its structure. In 1928 a passageway over top of the estuary was suggested, but it was not until 1959 that the commitment of the authorities was obtained in order to authorize construction. Finally, work began in 1972 on this suspension bridge which would only be concluded, after numerous inconveniences, in 1981 with the inauguration of the Humber River Bridge, the third longest in the world.

D epuis la fin du 19ème siècle, il était nécessaire de trouver un moyen de relier les deux rives de cet estuaire. Le premier projet remonte en effet à 1872, où l'on suggère la construction d'un tunnel, qui s'avère irréalisable à cause du coût trop élevé du projet. Déjà en 1928, un plan de construction est établi pour passer au-dessus de l'estuaire, mais il faudra attendre 1959 avant que les autorités donnent leur accord pour son exécution. Finalement, les travaux débutent en 1972 et après de nombreuses difficultés, ce pont suspendu est officiellement inauguré en 1981 sous le nom d'Humber River Bridge, le troisième plus grand du monde.

S eit Ende des 19. Jahrhunderts stellte man bereits Überlegungen zur möglichen Verbindung der beiden Ufer der Trichtermündung des Humber an. Im Jahr 1872 plante man den Bau eines Tunnels, der allerdings wegen zu hoher Kosten verworfen wurde. Bereits seit 1928 bestand das Projekt zum Bau einer Brücke, doch erst 1959 wurde diesem endgültig zugestimmt. Die Bauarbeiten begannen 1972 und dauerten bis zum Jahr 1981, als nach der Überwindung ständig auftretender Probleme und Schwierigkeiten endlich die drittlängste Hängebrücke der Welt eingeweiht werden konnte.

The fundamental necessity for the existence of a connection between the two shores of the estuary was sufficient to overcome all the setbacks in this project. Although construction lasted for several years, its opening to public use was achieved in 1981.

Le besoin fondamental d'assurer une liaison entre les deux rives de l'estuaire prévaut sur les inconvénients que le projet comporte. Bien que la construction se prolonge pendant plusieurs années, il est ouvert au public dès 1981.

Die absolute Notwendigkeit der Verbindung der Ufer der Trichtermündung des Humber siegte über die Schwierigkeiten, die dieses Projekt aufwarf. Der Bau zog sich über Jahre hin und wurde 1981 endlich fertiggestellt.

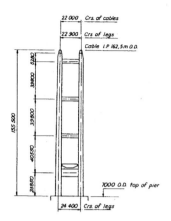

```
22 000   Crs. of cables
22 900   Crs of legs
         Cable  I.P 162,5m O.D.
820
39800
155 500
39800
40550
28850
         7000 O.D. top of pier
24 400   Crs. of legs
```

ELEVATION OF TOWERS

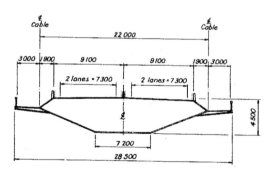

```
ℓ Cable                                    ℓ Cable
              22 000
3000  1800    9 100         9 100      1900  3000
      2 lanes = 7.300   2 lanes = 7.300
                    ℓ                          4.500
              7 200
              28 500
```

The work began in 1972 with the construction of the towers. Their location was of great importance in order to provide the greatest open space possible for navigation. In this manner, and with but one sole support in the water, 30 metres of clearance were gained for navigation.

Les travaux commencent par la construction des tours en 1972, dont la position est capitale pour pouvoir conserver la plus grande distance libre de navigation. Ce pont est composé d'un espace libre de 30 mètres de hauteur avec un seul point d'appui sur l'eau.

Die Bauarbeiten begannen 1972 mit der Errichtung der Türme, deren Standort von großer Bedeutung für den Erhalt der maximalen Freiheit für den Schiffsverkehr waren. Es befindet sich nur ein Brückenpfeiler im Wasser und die Plattform in 30 m Höhe.

The design of a suspension bridge was carefully studied along with other typologies; nonetheless the construction of a bridge of this structural type turned out to be the most suitable due to the various conditions of the project, both in terms of cost as well as viability of the design.

Le schéma du pont suspendu a été soigneusement étudié, parmi d'autres typologies. La construction de cette structure particulière s'avère être la plus adéquate par rapport aux conditions du projet, tant du point de vue financier que pour la fiabilité de la conception.

Das Schema einer Hängebrücke wurde zusammen mit anderen möglichen Strukturen genauestens studiert und stellte sich als ideal für den technischen und den finanziellen Rahmen dieses Projekts heraus.

Kobe Naruto Route

Honshu-Shikoku Bridge Authority

HONSHU–SHIKOKU, JAPAN. 1976-1998

Length / Longueur / Gesamtlänge 89000 m.

This route, one of three in existence in the area, joins the islands of Honshu, Awaji and Shikoku in the east and is also known as the Kobe – Awaji – Naruto Expressway. Both commercial and cultural interchanges in the west of Japan have improved due to the construction of these bridges. The route begins in Kobe on the island of Honshu and heads towards Naruto on the island of Shikoku, passing over the island of Awaji and crossing two straits: the four-kilometres-wide Akashi Strait, and the Strait of Naruto with a width of 1.3 km. Two important bridges make up this route: the Ohnaruto (1976-1985) and the Akashi Kaikyo (1988-1998), both of which are typologically based on the design of the suspension bridge.

Cette route, qui figure parmi les trois qui existent dans cette zone, rattache par l'est les îles de Honshu, Awaji et Shikoku. Elle est également connue sous le nom de Kobe – Awaji – Naruto Expressway. Sa construction a facilité les échanges commerciaux et culturels dans l'Ouest du Japon. Cette route va de Kobe, dans l'île de Honshu, jusqu'à Naruto, dans l'île de Shikoku, en passant par l'île d'Awaji et en traversant deux détroits : Akashi, de 4 km de large, et celui de Naruto, de 1,3 km. Elle est formée de deux ponts: l'Ohnaruto (1976-1985) et l'Akashi Kaikyo (1988-1998), basés sur la typologie du pont suspendu.

Diese Strecke, eine der drei in diesem Gebiet bestehenden, verbindet die Inseln Honshu, Awaji und Shikoku und ist auch als der Kobe – Awaji – Naruto Expressway bekannt. Mit ihrem Bau wurde der kommerzielle und kulturelle Austausch innerhalb des Westens Japans ermöglicht. Die Route beginnt in Kobe auf der Insel Honshu, verläuft über die Insel Awaji und endet in Naruto auf der Insel Shikoku. Dabei überqueren zwei Brücken zwei Meerengen: die von Akashimit 4 km Breite und dievon Naruto mit 1,3 km Breite. Die beiden Hängebrücken wurden Ohnaruto (1976-1985) und Akashi Kaikyo (1988-1998) genannt.

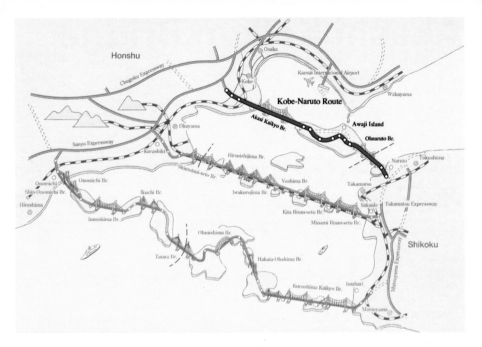

Kobe-Naruto Route

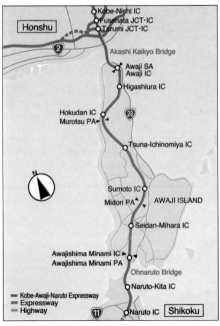

Honshu

- Kobe-Nishi IC
- Fusehata JCT·IC
- Tarumi JCT·IC

Akashi Kaikyo Bridge

- Awaji SA / Awaji IC
- Higashiura IC

Hokudan IC / Murotsu PA

- Tsuna-Ichinomiya IC

Sumoto IC / Midori PA — AWAJI ISLAND

- Seidan-Mihara IC

Awajishima Minami IC / Awajishima Minami PA

Ohnaruto Bridge

- Naruto-Kita IC
- Naruto IC — Shikoku

Legend:
- Kobe-Awaji-Naruto Expressway
- Expressway
- Highway

The Kobe – Naruto Route, one of the three principal connections between the islands of Honshu and Shikoku, is formed by two suspension bridges which belong to the Honshu-Shikoku Bridge Authority. The construction of each of the two bridges took approximately 10 years.

La route Kobe – Naruto, une des trois connexions principales entre les îles de Honshu et Shikoku, est constituée de deux des ponts suspendus qui appartiennent aux autorités de Honshu-Shikoku Bridge. La construction a pris environ 10 ans pour chacun des ponts.

Die Route Kobe – Naruto, eine der drei wichtigsten Verbindungen zwischen den Inseln Honshu und Shikoku, besteht aus zwei Hängebrücken, die der Honshu-Shikoku Bridge Authority gehören. Der Bau jeder einzelnen Brücke dauerte etwa 10 Jahre.

Akashi Kaikyo Bridge

Length / Longueur / Gesamtlänge 3911 m.
Span / Travée / Hauptspannweite 1991 m.

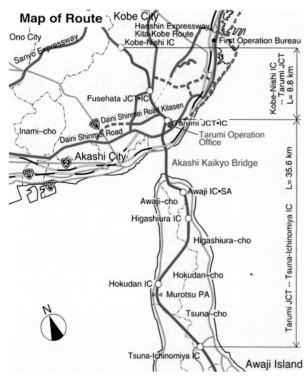

Map of Route

Kobe City
Hanshin Expressway
Kita-Kobe Route
Kobe-Nishi IC
First Operation Bureau
Ono City
Sanyo Expressway
Fusehata JCT·IC
Daini Shinmei Road Kitasen
Daini Shinmei Road
Inami–cho
Tarumi JCT·IC
Tarumi Operation Office
Akashi City
Akashi Kaikyo Bridge
Awaji IC·SA
Awaji–cho
Higashiura IC
Higashiura–cho
Hokudan–cho
Hokudan IC
Murotsu PA
Tsuna–cho
Tsuna-Ichinomiya IC
Awaji Island

Kobe-Nishi IC -- Tarumi JCT L= 8.8 km
Tarumi JCT -- Tsuna-Ichinomiya IC L = 35.6 km

The Akashi Kaikyo Bridge, with 6 lanes in use, is currently the longest suspension bridge in the world. It surpasses the Humber River Bridge (also included in this monograph) —with its centre span of 1410 m. and constructed between 1972 and 1981 in England— by 581 m.

Le pont Akashi Kaikyo, avec 6 voies de dépassement, est actuellement le pont suspendu le plus long du monde, dépassant de 581 m l'Humber Bridge (également inclus dans cet ouvrage), pont construit entre 1972 et 1981 en Angleterre, avec une travée centrale de 1410 m.

Die Akashi Kaikyo, mit sechs Fahrbahnen, ist im Moment die längste Hängebrücke der Welt und überbietet die Humber Bridge, deren Hauptspannweite 1410 m misst und die von 1972 bis 1981 in England erbaut wurde (auch in dieser Sammlung aufgeführt), um 581 m.

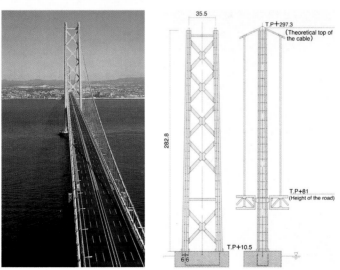

35.5

282.8

T.P+297.3
（Theoretical top of
the cable）

T.P+81
(Height of the road)

T.P+10.5

6.6

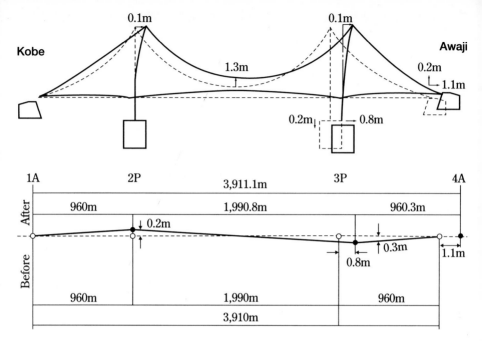

Kobe ... **Awaji**

0.1m 0.1m
1.3m
0.2m
1.1m
0.2m → 0.8m

1A	2P	3,911.1m	3P	4A

After

960m   1,990.8m   960.3m

↓ 0.2m

↑ 0.3m
0.8m   1.1m

Before

960m   1,990m   960m

3,910m

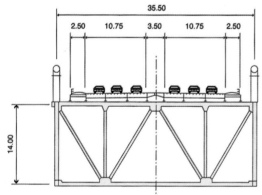

35.50
2.50 10.75 3.50 10.75 2.50
14.00

In 1995 while still in construction, the structure of the bridge suffered the battering of earthquake Hanshin. Although both the length (3911 m.) and the centre span (1991 m.) were increased by 1 m. over those originally planned, the structure in general suffered no adverse consequences.

En 1995, alors qu'elle est en travaux, la structure subit les secousses du tremblement de terre Hanshin. Malgré l'augmentation d'un mètre de la longueur (3911 m) et de la travée centrale (1991 m) suivant le projet d'origine, la structure générale échappe aux conséquences de ce tremblement de terre.

Im Jahr 1995, mitten im Bau der Brücke, schockte das Erdbeben Hanshin Japan. Obwohl die Gesamtlänge (3911 m) und dieHauptspannweite (1991 m) dadurch um jeweils 1 m länger wurden als ursprünglich geplant, hat die Gesamtstruktur nicht unter den Folgen des Bebens gelitten.

In the original project the deck was planned to include a railway line, but in 1985 the decision was made to restrict the passage and limit its use to motor vehicles.

Dans le projet original, la plate-forme devait comprendre une voie ferrée, mais en 1985, on choisit de réduire le passage et d'en faire exclusivement une autoroute.

Das Originalprojekt sah auch eine Eisenbahnschiene auf der Plattform der Brücke vor, aber 1985 wurde entschieden den Bau lediglich auf eine Autobahn zu beschränken.

Ohnaruto Bridge

Length / Longueur / Gesamtlänge 1629 m.
Span / Travée / Hauptspannweite 876 m.

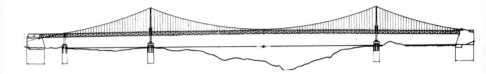

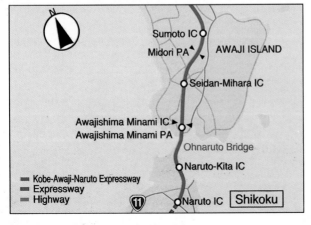

The Ohnaruto Bridge (1976 - 1985) was the first bridge built on the Kobe – Naruto Route. Its structural design is based on the suspension bridge with a total length of 1629 m. and a centre span of 876 m.

Le pont Ohnaruto (1976 - 1985) fut l'un des premiers ponts construits sur la route Kobe – Naruto. Sa structure est celle du pont suspendu, d'une longueur totale de 1629 m et d'une travée centrale de 876 m.

Die Ohnaruto (1976 - 1985) wurde als erste der Kobe – Naruto Route fertiggestellt. Die Hängebrücke misst eine Gesamtlänge von 1629 m und eine Hauptspannweite von 876 m.

This bridge upon the Strait of Naruto is responsible for joining the islands of Awaji and Shikoku. On account of the seismic and wind conditions in the area, a study of its structural stability was fundamental during the development of the project.

La fonction de ce pont, situé sur le détroit de Naruto, est de relier les îles d'Awaji et de Shikoku. Dû aux conditions sismiques et venteuses de la région, des études approfondies de la stabilité de la structure sont menées pendant tout le développement du projet.

Diese Brücke über der Meerenge von Naruto verbindet die Inseln Awaji und Shikoku. Wegen der seismischen Bewegungen und der starken Winde in dieser Region waren die Berechnungen zur Stabilität der Brücke vor und während des Baus besonders wichtig.

Onomichi-Imabari Route

Honshu-Shikoku Bridge Authority

HONSHU-SHIKOKU, JAPAN. 1976-1999

Length / Longueur / Gesamtlänge 59000 m.

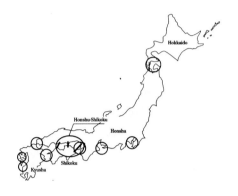

U pon termination of this route, the project, initiated in 1975 for the development of three connections between the islands of Honshu and Shikoku, came to a conclusion. In this case this western connection begins at Onomichi on the island of Honshu and heads towards Imabari on the island of Shikoku. The completed route, also known as the Nishi-Seto Expressway, joins 7 islands and is formed by10 bridges of various different structural typologies: Omishima (1976-1979), Innoshima (1977-1983), Hakata-Oshima (1981-1988), Ikuchi (1986-1991), Tatara (1990-1999), the 3 Kurushima Kaikyo Bridges (1990-1999) and the Shin Onomichi Bridge (1996-1999).

L' achèvement de cette route marque la conclusion du projet de développement de trois lignes de communication entre les îles de Honshu et Shikoku initié en 1975. Cette route rattache Onomichi dans l'île de Honshu, à Imabari, dans l'île de Shikoku, cette fois par l'ouest. Egalement connue sous le nom de Nishi–Seto Expressway, elle assure la connexion de 7 îles et comporte 10 ponts de diverses structures : Omishima (1976-1979), Innoshima (1977-1983), Hakata-Oshima (1981-1988), Ikuchi (1986-1991), Tatara (1990-1999), les 3 ponts de Kurushima Kaikyo (1990-1999) et Shin Onomichi (1996-1999).

Mit der Fertigstellung dieser Route wurde das 1975 begonnene Projekt zur Erstellung von drei Verbindungswegen zwischen den Inseln Honshu und Shikoku vollendet. Der Übergang führt in Richtung Westen, beginnend in Onomichi auf der Insel Honshu bis nach Imabari auf der Insel Shikoku. Diese Route, die auch als Nishi – Seto Expressway bekannt ist, verbindet insgesamt sieben Inseln und besteht aus zehn Brücken unterschiedlicher Bauweisen: die Omishima (1976-1979), Innoshima (1977-1983), Hakata-Oshima (1981-1988), Ikuchi (1986-1991), Tatara (1990-1999), die drei Brücken des Kurushima Kaikyo (1990-1999) und die Shin Onomichi (1996-1999).

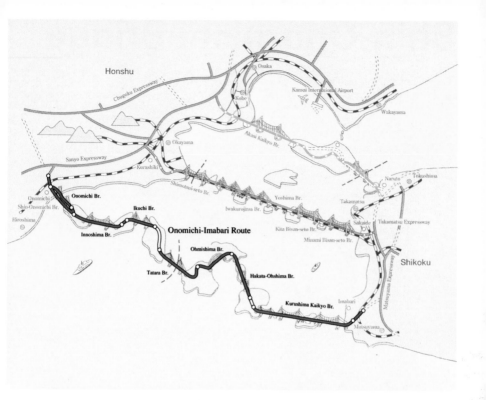

Shin-Onomichi Bridge

Length / Longueur / Gesamtlänge 546 m.
Span / Travée / Hauptspannweite 215 m.

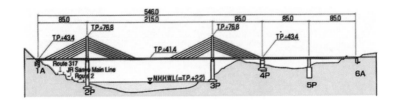

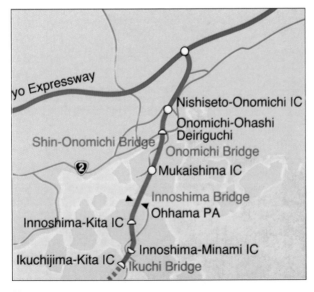

The Shin Onomichi Bridge (1996-1999) has a total length of 546 m., a centre span of 215 m. and towers of 77 m. in height. The structure, of metal and concrete, is based on the design of the cable-stayed bridge.

Le pont Shin Onomichi (1996-1999) mesure 546 m de long; sa travée centrale est de 215 m, et ses tours s'élèvent jusqu'à 77 m. La structure, alliant métal et béton, est basée sur le schéma du pont à haubans.

Die Brücke Shin Onomichi (1996 – 1999) misst eine Gesamtlänge von 546 m, eine Hauptspannweite von 215 m und eine Turmhöhe von 77 m. Der Metall und Betonbau entspricht dem strukturellen Schema einer Schrägseilbrücke.

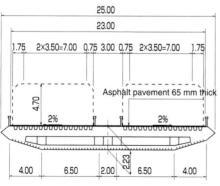

The design of this bridge is similar to that of the old Onomichi Bridge and is built 55 m. away from the original. For this reason its formal image was also inspired by the existing bridge. Thus the new pair of bridges blend together in harmonious fashion to form a new unity.

La conception de ce pont est semblable à celle de l'ancien pont Onomichi, et il se situe à 55 m de distance seulement, car son image formelle est également inspirée de l'original. Ainsi, ces deux ponts se complètent harmonieusement pour former une nouvelle unité.

Diese Brücke gleicht im Design der alten Onomichi und wurde in einer Entfernung von nur 55 m von dieser errichtet. Auf diese Weise verschmilzt das Brückenpaar auf harmonische Weise und bildet eine neue Einheit.

Innoshima Bridge

Length / Longueur / Gesamtlänge 1270 m.
Span / Travée / Hauptspannweite 770 m.

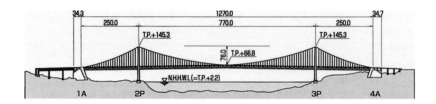

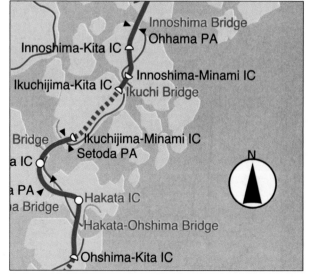

The Innoshima Bridge (1977-1983) has a total length of 1270 m. and a centre span of 770 m., with towers 145 m. high. The structure, of metal and concrete, is based on the design of the suspension bridge.

La longueur totale du pont Innoshima (1977-1983) est de 1270 m, sa travée centrale, de 770 m, et ses tours, 145 m. La structure de métal et de béton respecte le modèle du pont suspendu.

Die Innoshima (1977-1983) ist insgesamt 1270 m lang, hat eine Hauptspannweite von 770 m und Türme mit einer Höhe von 145 m. Die Brücke wurde aus Metall und Beton gebaut und entspricht in ihrer Bauweise der einer Hängebrücke.

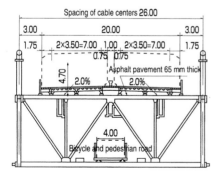

Spacing of cable centers 26.00

3.00 20.00 3.00

1.75 2×3.50=7.00 1.00 2×3.50=7.00 1.75

0.75 0.75

4.70 2.0% 2.0% Asphalt pavement 65 mm thick

4.00

Bicycle and pedestrian road

The construction of this bridge marked a milestone within the project of the three routes joining the islands. It was the first suspension bridge and in its design certain considerations were taken which would later become firmly established in the other structures of these routes.

La construction de ce pont marque une étape cruciale du projet des trois routes entre les îles. Pendant l'élaboration de ce premier pont suspendu, on prend déjà en considération de futures consolidations grâce à d'autres structures routières.

Der Bau dieser Brücke stellte einen Meilenstein innerhalb des Projekts der drei Routen dar. Es war die erste Hängebrücke und die gesammelten Erfahrungen bei ihrer Planung und Errichtung waren eine wichtige Stütze bei dem Bau späterer Strukturen.

Ikuchi Bridge

Length / Longueur / Gesamtlänge 790 m.
Span / Travée / Hauptspannweite 490 m.

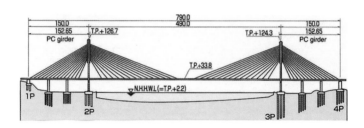

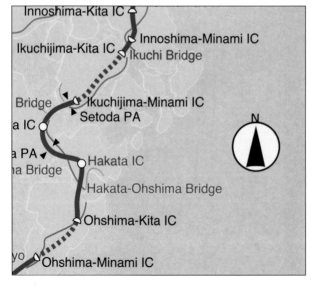

The Ikuchi Bridge (1986-1991) has a total length of 790 m., a centre span of 490 m. and towers 127 m. high. The structure, composed of metal and concrete, is based on the cable-stayed bridge design.

Le pont Ikuchi (1986-1991) a une longueur totale de 790 m, une travée centrale de 490 m et des tours de 127 m de hauteur. La structure, composée de métal et de béton, se base sur le modèle du pont à haubans.

Die Ikuchi (1986-1991) misst insgesamt 790 m, ihre Hauptspannweite 490 m und ihre Türme eine Höhe von 127 m. Die aus Metall und Beton bestehende Struktur wurde im Stil einer Schrägseilbrücke errichtet.

Steel girder (center span)

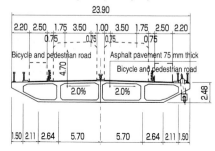

New methods, for both the optimization of the materials used as well as seismic control of the structure as a whole, were developed for the construction of this bridge. It would be the first step towards the future development of more complex structures.

Des nouvelles méthodes ont été développées pour la construction de ce pont, tant au niveau de l'exploitation des matériaux que des contrôles sismiques, premier pas du développement ultérieur de structures plus complexes.

Beim Bau dieser Brücke wurden neue Methoden entwickelt, die eine optimalere Nutzung der Baumaterialien und eine bessere seismische Kontrolle ermöglichten. Die Ikuchi war Grundlage für den Bau späterer komplexerer Strukturen.

Tatara Bridge

Length / Longueur / Gesamtlänge 1480 m.
Span / Travée / Hauptspannweite 890 m.

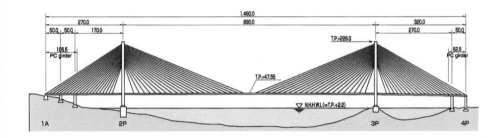

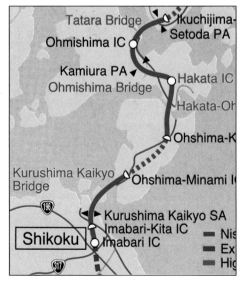

The Tatara Bridge (1990-1999) has a total length of 1480 m., a centre span of 890 m. and towers of 226 m. in height. The structure, a combination of metal and concrete, is based on the cable-stayed bridge design.

Le pont Tatara (1990-1999) a une longueur totale de 1480 m, une travée centrale de 890 m et des tours de 226 m. La structure, composée de métal et de béton, se base sur le modèle du pont à haubans.

Die Gesamtlänge der Tatara (1990-1999) beträgt 1480 m während ihre Hauptspannweite 890 m und ihre Türme 226 m messen. Die Schrägseilbrücke wurde aus Metall und Beton errichtet.

Steel girder (center span)

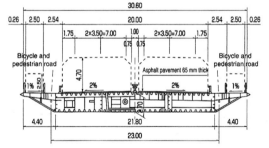

30.60

0.26 | 2.50 | 2.54 | 20.00 | 2.54 | 2.50 | 0.26

1.75 | 2×3.50=7.00 | 1.00 | 2×3.50=7.00 | 1.75
0.75 0.75

Bicycle and pedestrian road — Bicycle and pedestrian road

4.70

Asphalt pavement 65 mm thick

1% 2.50 | 2% | 2% | 1%

4.40 | 21.80 | 4.40

23.00

PC girder (side span)

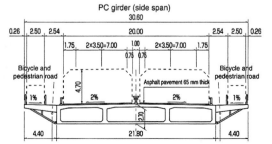

30.60

0.26 | 2.50 | 2.54 | 20.00 | 2.54 | 2.50 | 0.26

1.75 | 2×3.50=7.00 | 1.00 | 2×3.50=7.00 | 1.75
0.75 0.75

Bicycle and pedestrian road — Bicycle and pedestrian road

4.70

Asphalt pavement 65 mm thick

1% | 2% | 2% | 1%

2.70

4.40 | 21.80 | 4.40

This bridge became the longest cable-stayed bridge in the world, supplanting the Normandie Bridge (also included in this monograph), which has a centre span of 856 m. and was built in France between 1992 and 1995.

Ce pont est devenu le pont à haubans le plus long du monde, supplantant le pont de Normandie (également inclus dans cet ouvrage), construit en France entre 1992 et 1995, d'une travée centrale de 856 m.

Die Tatara wurde zur längsten Schrägseilbrücke der Welt und verwies die Brücke der Normandie in Frankreich (auch in dieser Sammlung erwähnt), die zwischen 1992 und 1995 erbaut wurde und über einen Hauptspannweite von 856 m verfügt, auf den zweiten Platz.

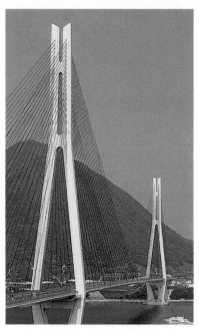

Omishima Bridge

Length / Longueur / Gesamtlänge 328 m.
Span / Travée / Hauptspannweite 297 m.

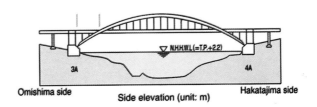

NHHWL.(=T.P.+2.2)

3A   4A

Omishima side   Side elevation (unit: m)   Hakatajima side

The Omishima Bridge (1976-1979) has a to**
length of 328 m. and a centre span of 297 **
The structure combines the use of steel a**
concrete is based on the design of the ar**
bridge, the only such bridge on all the isla**
routes.

Le pont Omishima (1976-1979) mesure 328
de long, et sa travée centrale est de 297 m.
structure est un mélange d'acier et de béto
le seul pont de type arc de toutes les rout

Die Omishima (1976-1979) misst insgesamt ei
Länge von 328 m und eine Hauptspannweite v
297 m. Diese Brücke ist die einzige Bogenbrüc
der gesamten drei Routen und wurde ebenfa
aus Metall und Beton gebaut.

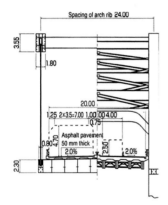

Spacing of arch rib 24.00

3.55

1.80

20.00
1.25 2×3.5=7.00 1.00 1.00 4.00
0.75
Asphalt pavement
0.80 50 mm thick
4.70 2.0% 2.50 2.0%
2.30

A pair of arches joined by ribs constitute the basis of the structure of this bridge which is in charge of connecting the islands of Omishima, Hanaguriseto and Hakatajima. Upon its inauguration it became the longest bridge in the region.

Deux arcs reliés par des nervures forment la base structurale de ce pont, chargé de relier les îles Omishima, Hanaguriseto et Hakatajima. Il représente au moment de son inauguration l'un des plus grands ponts de la région.

Zwei durch Rippen verbundene Bögen bilden die Basis dieser Brückenstruktur, die die Inseln Omishima, Hanaguriseto und Hakatajima verbindet. Bei ihrer Einweihung wurde sie zur längsten Brücke der Gegend.

Hakata Oshima Bridge

HAKATA: Length / Longueur / Gesamtlänge 325 m.
        Span / Travée / Hauptspannweite 145 m.

OSHIMA: Length / Longueur / Gesamtlänge 840 m.
        Span / Travée / Hauptspannweite 560 m.

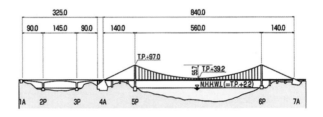

The Hakata Bridge (1981-1988) has a total length of 325 m. and a centre span of 145 m. The Oshima Bridge, on the other hand, is 840 m. long with a centre span of 560 m. The two structures together are known as the Hakata Oshima Bridge.

Les mesures du pont Hakata (1981-1988) sont les suivantes : 325 m pour la longueur, et 145 m pour la travée centrale. L'Oshima, quant à lui, mesure 840 m de long, avec une travée centrale de 560 m. Les deux structures sont connues sous le nom de pont Hakata Oshima.

Die Länge der Brücke Hakata (1981-1988) beträgt 325 m und die ihrer Hauptspannweite 145 m. Die Oshima ist bedeutend länger und misst bei einer Hauptspannweite von 560 m insgesamt 840 m. Die beiden Strukturen sind unter dem Namen Hakata-Oshima-Brücke bekannt.

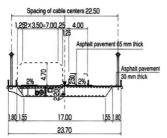

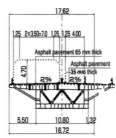

These two bridges are responsible for connecting the islands of Hakatajima and Michikajima (Hakata) with the island of Oshima (Oshima). The Hakata Bridge consists of a continuous metallic deck with three supports while the Oshima Bridge is a suspension bridge.

Ces deux ponts relient les îles Hakatajima et Michikajima (Hakata) à celle d'Oshima (Oshima). Le Hakata est constitué d'une plate-forme métallique avec trois points d'appui, et Oshima est un pont suspendu.

Die beiden Brücken verbinden die Inseln Hakatajima und Michikajima (Hakata) mit der Insel Oshima (Oshima). Die Hakata besteht aus einer durchgehenden Metallplattform mit drei Pfeilern und die Oshima ist eine Hängebrücke.

Kurushima Kaikyo Bridge

N°1: Length / Longueur / Gesamtlänge 960 m.
Span / Travée / Hauptspannweite 600 m.

N°2: Length / Longueur / Gesamtlänge 1570 m.
Span / Travée / Hauptspannweite 1020 m.

N°3: Length / Longueur / Gesamtlänge 1570 m.
Span / Travée / Hauptspannweite 1030 m.

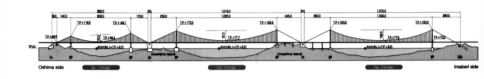

The Kurushima Kaikyo Bridge (1990-1999) is made up of three structures of differing lengths: 960 m. (bridge no. 1), 1515 m. (bridge no. 2) and 1570 m. (bridge no. 3). The centre spans measure 600 m., 1020 m. and 1030 m. respectively.

Kurushima Kaikyo (1990-1999) est formé de trois structures de différentes longueurs : 960 m (1er pont), 1515 m (2ème pont) et 1570 m (3ème pont). Les travées centrales mesurent 600, 1020 et 1030 m respectivement.

Die Kurushima Kaikyo (1990-1999) besteht aus drei Einheiten unterschiedlicher Längen: 960 m (Brücke Nr. 1), 1515 m (Brücke Nr. 2) und 1570 m (Brücke Nr. 3). Die Länge der Hauptspannweiten beträgt jeweils 600 m, 1020 m und 1030 m.

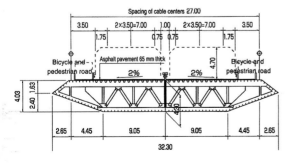

Spacing of cable centers 27.00

3.50 | 2×3.50=7.00 | 1.00 | 2×3.50=7.00 | 3.50

1.75 | 0.75 0.75 | 1.75

Bicycle and – pedestrian road | Asphalt pavement 65 mm thick | 4.70 | Bicycle and pedestrian road

2% | 2% | 4.50

4.03 | 2.40 | 1.63

2.65 | 4.45 | 9.05 | 9.05 | 4.45 | 2.65

32.30

The three structures –which are joined to each other– have the suspension bridge as their basic design. They are responsible for connecting the islands of Oshima and Imabari, across the dangerous Kurushima Strait.

Le schéma de ces trois structures (reliées entre elles) est celui du pont suspendu. Elles relient les îles d'Oshima et d'Imabari par le périlleux détroit de Kurushima.

Die drei Strukturen, die untereinander verbunden sind, wurden im Stil von Hängebrücken erbaut und verbinden die Inseln Oshima und Imabari über die gefährliche Meerenge von Kurushima.

103

Rheinbrücke Speyer

W. Tiedje, arq.; Louis Wintergerst, ing.

August Klönne, DSD Dillinger Stahlbau GmbH,
Grün & Bilfinger

SPEYER, DEUTSCHLAND. 1977

Length / Longueur / Gesamtlänge 456 m.
Span / Travée / Hauptspannweite 275 m.

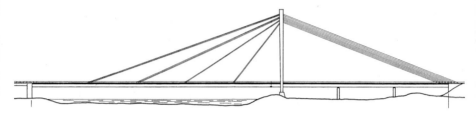

This bridge was built to cross the Rhine River as it flows through the city of Speyer and forms a part of the A61 Krefeld-Ludwigshafen-Speyer Highway. The structure is typologically based on the cable-stayed bridge, which in this case uses metallic elements with one single pylon from which the cables which sustain the deck are suspended. As a result of its design, the ensemble composed of the tower-and-cables unit forms a natural border separating the two traffic directions. Thanks to careful study of its structuring this bridge succeeds in crossing the river without the necessity of any supports within the water, while at the same time attaining a deck 33 m. wide.

Ce pont a pour fonction la traversée de la rivière Rin sur son chemin vers la ville de Speyer ; il fait partie de la voie rapide A61 Krefeld-Ludwigshafen-Speyer. Sa structure est basée sur la typologie du pont à haubans, qui dans ce cas comporte des éléments métalliques et une tour unique où se regroupent les haubans qui soutiennent la plate-forme. Sa conception fait de cet ensemble formé par une tour-haubans une frontière naturelle entre les deux sens de circulation. L'étude de la structure a permis de traverser la rivière sans avoir recours à des appuis, ce qui donne une plate-forme de 33 m de large.

Diese Brücke überquert den Rhein innerhalb der Stadt Speyer und bildet Teil der Autobahn A61 Krefeld-Ludwigshafen-Speyer. Ihre Bauweise entspricht der einer Schrägseilbrücke, die mit metallischen Elementen errichtet wurde und über nur einen Turm verfügt der alle Seile, die zur Befestigung der Plattform nötig sind, hält. Die Brücke wurde so entworfen, dass die Seile gleichzeitig eine Fahrtrichtung von der entgegengesetzten trennen und eine natürliche Barriere bilden. Dank der in diesem Fall angewandten Struktur hat man erreicht, den Fluss mit einer 33 m breiten Plattform zu überbrücken ohne in ihm selbst Befestigungselemente anzubringen.

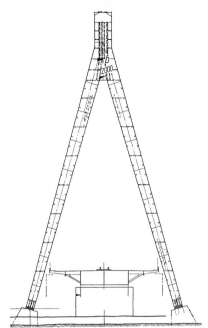

The design of the pylon is of fundamental importance as it constitutes the main visual reference of the project. Thus this slender and unique pylon, along with the cables, forms the most meticulous piece of the ensemble. This pair also intervenes as the border separating different lanes of traffic.

La conception de la tour est l'élément essentiel à ce pont, en ce qu'il constitue la référence visuelle du projet. Ainsi, cette tour allongée et unique forme, de pair avec les traverses, la pièce la plus soignée de l'ensemble. Ces deux éléments agissent aussi comme séparation entre les deux voies.

Das Design des Turms ist von großer Bedeutung für das Erscheinungsbild dieses Projekts. Darum wird dieser elegante und einzigartige Turm und dessen Seile besonders gepflegt. Die Seile grenzen gleichzeitig die beiden Fahrtrichtungen voneinander ab.

109

Krummbach Bridge

Paul Missbauer, ing.

NATIONALE N° 9, SUISSE. 1978

Length / Longueur / Gesamtlänge 621 m.
Span / Travée / Hauptspannweite 124 m.

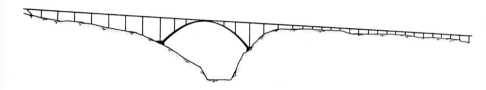

The routing of a new group of highways near the Swiss-Italian border required a passage over the Krummbach Mountains. The idea of using the arch for the bridge's structural system arose out of this pass over the valley. This technique, although the subject of lengthy discussion due to its cost, was nonetheless the most suitable solution. A detailed study of the construction process succeeded in maintaining the original cost of the project. The work was carried out in three phases and required the use of provisional auxiliary structures which would facilitate the construction of the arches as well as provide for a constant control of the stability of the structure as a whole.

Le plan d'un nouvel ensemble de routes près de la frontière suisse–italienne incluait la nécessité de franchir les montagnes Krummbach. Du passage à travers la vallée est née l'idée d'utiliser l'arc comme base structurelle du pont. Cette technique, longuement disputée pour son coût élevé, était toutefois la plus appropriée, et une étude détaillée de la procédure de construction permit de réduire les frais du projet. La construction comprend plusieurs phases de développement, et des structures auxiliaires provisoires sont nécessaires afin de faciliter la construction des arcs et de contrôler en permanence la stabilité de la structure de l'ensemble.

Der Bau einer neuen Straßengruppe nah der schweizerisch – italienischen Grenze brachte die Notwendigkeit die Krummbach Berge zu überbrücken mit sich. Der von vielen gewünschte Bau einer Bogenbrücke wurde wegen seiner hohen Kosten lange diskutiert. Durch die gute Planung des Projekts hielten sich die Ausgaben allerdings in Grenzen und die Brücke konnte in dem für diesen Fall idealen Stil gebaut werden. Bei dem Bauder Brückewares notwendig, provisorische Hilfsstrukturen zu errichten um den Bogenbauzu erleichtern und kontinuierlich die Stabilität der Gesamtstruktur zu überwachen.

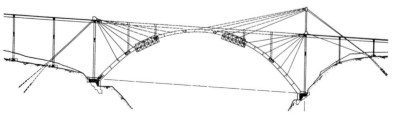

The construction of an auxiliary structure which would later be withdrawn facilitated the execution of the project while at the same time providing constant control over the rigidity of the new structure and its tensioning process.

La construction d'une structure auxiliaire, ensuite retirée, a contribué à la bonne exécution de l'œuvre, permettant de contrôler à tout moment à la fois la rigidité de la nouvelle structure et son procédé de mise en tension.

Der Errichtung von Hilfsstrukturen, die später wieder entfernt wurden, erleichterte den Bau dieses Werks um ein Vielfaches und erlaubte eine ständige Kontrolle der Stabilität der neuen Brücke während des Spannungsprozesses.

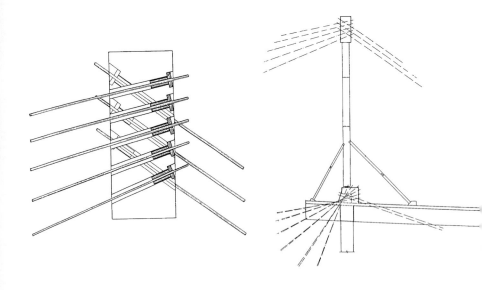

On account of the difference in level between the two slopes of the valley, each side of the arches finishes at a different height. A group of ribs joining the arches together lends greater stiffness to the structure.

Dû à la différence de niveau entre un point et un autre de la vallée, chaque extrémité des arcs a une hauteur différente. Un ensemble de nervures relie les arcs entre eux, donnant plus de rigidité à la structure.

Der Höhenunterschied der beiden Seiten des Tals führte dazu, dass die Bögen ebenfalls in verschiedenen Höhen angelegt wurden. Die Bögen werden außerdem durch Rippen verbunden, die der Struktur zusätzliche Stabilität geben.

117

Sancho El Mayor

Carlos Fernández Casado, ing.
Javier Manterola Armisen, Leonardo Fernández Troyano, ing

NAVARRA, ESPAÑA. 1978
Span / Travée / Hauptspannweite 146,30 m.

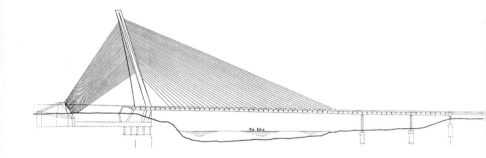

Rio Ebro

The Sancho El Mayor Bridge exists as part of the highway network of Navarra at its crossing over the Ebro River. The proposed structure is based on a single pylon which received all the care and attention of the design. This concrete pylon, slender and elegant, was erected as the centre of attention without nonetheless obstructing traffic nor wind currents in any way. One of its peculiarities is the three groups of cables attached to it: two are directed towards lateral counterweights while the final group passes through the bridge's centre axis. The rigorous quality control of this structure required that it be capable of supporting a weight of 26 tonnes before opening it to public use.

Le pont Sancho el Mayor fait partie du réseau routier de Navarre et passe au-dessus de la rivière Ebre. Sa structure est constituée d'une tour unique, sur laquelle se sont centrés les efforts lors de la conception. Cette tour svelte et élégante en béton a été érigée comme le principal centre d'attention, sans qu'elle constitue un obstacle à la circulation ou au vent. Une de ses particularités réside dans les trois groupes de traverses qui arrivent jusqu'à la tour : deux rejoignent les contrepoids latéraux et le dernier passe par l'axe central du pont. Les stricts contrôles de qualité menés ont démontré que la structure pouvait supporter 26 tonnes avant son inauguration publique.

Als Teil des Straßennetzes von Navarra treffen wir auf die Brücke Sancho El Mayor über dem Ebro. Dem einzigen Turm ihrer Baustruktur wurde beim Design ganz besondere Aufmerksamkeit gewidmet. Dieser schlanke und elegante Turm aus Beton macht den Charakter der Brücke aus, ohne ein Hindernis weder für den Verkehr noch für den Wind darzustellen. Eine Besonderheit des Gebaus machen seine drei Seilgruppen aus: zwei von ihnen führen zu den seitlichen Gegengewichten und eine passiert die Zentralachse der Brücke. Die strengen Qualitätskontrollen schrieben vor, dass die Brücke bevor sie dem Publikumsverkehr geöffnet werden konnte, einem Test unterzogen werden musste, bei dem sie 26 Tonnen aushalten musste.

The three groups of cables attached to the pylon are distributed symmetrically, two groups are directed towards each of the lateral counter-weights while the third passes through the axis of the deck, thus constituting a natural lane divider.

Les trois groupes de haubans qui arrivent jusqu'à la tour sont symétriquement répartis, deux des groupes rejoignent chacun des contrepoids latéraux et l'autre groupe passe par l'axe de la plate-forme, où leur barrière naturelle sépare les voies.

Die drei Seilgruppen die am Turm befestigt sind, sind symmetrisch verteilt wurden, zwei von ihnen führen zu den seitlichen Gegenge-wichten und eine zur Achse der Plattform wobei sie gleichzeitig eine Barriere zwischen den Fahrbahnen darstellt

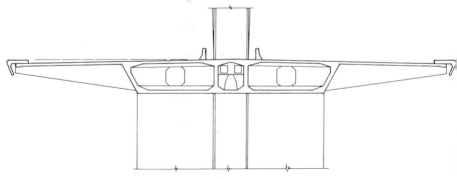

The most outstanding element in the design of this cable-stayed bridge is its pylon, which passes through the centre axis of the deck. This pylon has also become the focus of visual attention due to its position.

La tour, qui passe par l'axe de la plate-forme, est l'élément qui se détache le plus dans la conception de cet attrayant ensemble. La situation de celle-ci en fait également le centre d'attention visuel.

Das Design dieser Schrägseilbrücke hat den Turm, der sich auf der Achse der Plattform befindet, zum herausragender Element. Durch seine Stellung wird er auch zum visueller Zentrum des Gebaus.

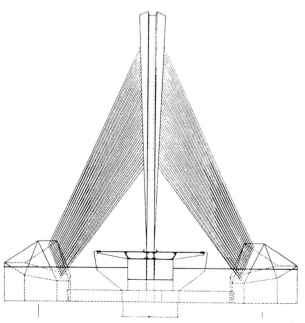

Kojima Sakaide Route

Honshu-Shikoku Bridge Authority

HONSHU-SHIKOKU, JAPAN. 1979-1988

Length / Longueur / Gesamtlänge 39000 m. / 32000 m.

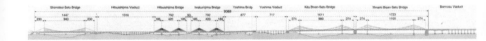

This is one of the three routes which cross the Seto Sea between the islands of Honshu and Shikoku. It passes through the centre of the islands and is also known as the Seto-Chuo Expressway & JR Seto-Ohashi Line. It offers both car and railway lanes, with a length of 39 km. and 32 km. respectively, over a two-level deck. Six structrures of different typologies make up this route: Kita Bisan-Seto (1979-1988), Minami Bisan-Seto (1979-1988), Shimotsui-Seto (1981-1988), Iwakurojima (1981-1988), Hitsuishijima (1982-1988) and Yosima (1983-1988). This series of bridges united together is known as the Seto-Ohashi Bridge.

Cette route compte parmi les trois qui relient les îles Honshu et Shikoku par la mer de Seto. Assurant la liaison à partir du centre de ces îles, elle est aussi connue comme la Seto-Chuo Expressway & JR Seto-Ohashi Line, d'une longueur de 39 et 32 km respectivement, et permet le passage de voitures et de trains grâce à des plates-formes à deux niveaux. Six structures de typologies variées forment cette route: Kita Bisan-Seto (1979-1988), Minami Bisan-Seto (1979-1988), Shimotsui-Seto (1981-1988), Iwakurojima (1981-1988), Hitsuishijima (1982- 1988), Yosima (1983-1988). Ces ponts sont regroupés sous le nom de Seto-Ohashi Bridge.

Diese Route ist eine der drei existierenden, die die Inseln Honshu und Shikoku über das Seto Binnenmeer verbindet. Die Strecke führt über die Zentren der Inseln und ist auch al Seto–Chuo Expressway & JR Seto–Ohashi Line bekannt. Sie ist 39 km lang und ermöglicht Autos und Zügen (32 km lange Strecke) über zweistöckige Plattformen die Überfahrt. Die Route besteht aus sechs Strukturen verschiedenen Konstruktionstyps: die Kita Bisan-Seto (1979-1988), Minami Bisan-Seto (1979-1988), Shimotsui-Seto (1981-1988), Iwakurojima (1981-1988), Hitsuishijima (1982-1988) und die Yosima (1983-1988). Die Gesamtheit dieser Brücken wird als die Seto-Ohashi Bridge bezeichnet.

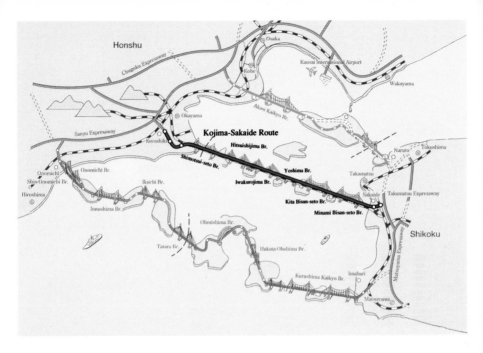

Honshu

Chugoku Expressway

Osaka

Kansai International Airport

Kobe

Wakayama

Sanyo Expressway

Okayama

Akasi Kaikyo Br.

Kurashiki

Kojima-Sakaide Route

Hitsuishijima Br.

Naruto   Tokushima

Shimotsui-seto Br.

Yoshima Br.

Takamatsu

Onomichi

Onomichi Br.

Ikuchi Br.

Iwakurojima Br.

Sakaide   Takamatsu Expressway

Shin-Onomichi Br.

Kita Bisan-seto Br.

Hiroshima

Innoshima Br.

Minami Bisan-seto Br.

Ohmishima Br.

Shikoku

Tatara Br.

Hakata-Ohshima Br.

Kurushima Kaikyo Br.

Imabari

Matsuyama Expressway

Matsuyama

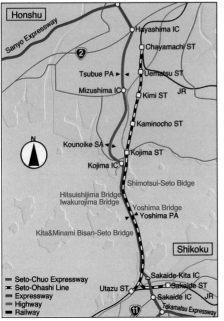

Honshu

Sanyo Expressway

2

Hayashima IC

Chayamachi ST

Tsubue PA

Uematsu ST

Mizushima IC

Kimi ST   JR

Kaminocho ST

Kounoike SA

Kojima ST

Kojima IC

Shimotsui-Seto Bidge

Hitsuishijima Bridge
Iwakurojima Bridge

Yoshima Bridge
Yoshima PA

Kita&Minami Bisan-Seto Bridge

Shikoku

Sakaide-Kita IC

Seto-Chuo Expressway
Seto-Ohashi Line
Expressway
Highway
Railway

Sakaide ST

Utazu ST   Sakaide IC   JR

11   Takamatsu Expressway

As a result of the demands of the physical characteristics of the region, a total of 18 bridges were built between the islands of Honshu and Shikoku between 1976 and 1999. These bridges divided into three routes over the Seto Sea are known as the Honshu-Shikoku Bridges.

Dû aux caractéristiques géographiques de la région, 18 ponts au total ont été construits entre 1976 et 1999 entre les îles Honshu et Shikoku, répartis en trois routes passant au-dessus de la mer Seto. Ils portent le nom de Honshu-Shikoku Bridges.

Wegen der physischen Eigenschaften dieser Region wurden in den Jahren 1976 bis 1999 zwischen den Inseln Honshu und Shikoku insgesamt 18 Brücken über das Seto-Binnenmeer gebaut. Sie sind als die Honshu-Shikoku Bridges bekannt.

Seto–Ohashi Bridge

The typology and centre span of the bridges vary in accordance with each case: the suspension bridges are Shimotsui-Seto (940 m), Kita Bisan-Seto (990 m.) and Minami Bisan-Seto (1100 m.) while Hitsuishijima (420 m.) and Iwakurojima (420 m.) are cable-stayed bridges.

La typologie et la travée centrale ne sont pas les mêmes pour les différents ponts : Shimotsui-Seto (940 m), Kita Bisan-Seto (990 m) et Minami Bisan-Seto (1100 m) sont des ponts suspendus, et Hitsuishijima (420 m) et Iwakurojima (420 m), des ponts à haubans.

Der Konstruktionstyp und die Hauptspannweite der Brücken variiert in jedem einzelnen der Fälle: die Shimotsui-Seto (940 m), Kita Bisan-Seto (990 m) und Minami Bisan-Seto (1100 m) sind Hängebrücken und die Hitsuishijima (420 m) und Iwakurojima (420 m) sind Schrägseilbrücken.

Seto–Ohashi Bridge

This bridge deck provides a passage for both a highway and railway line between the two islands. Although the desk itself is constructed on two levels throughout the entire route, the individual bridges follow a variety of designs such as the suspension or cable-stayed bridge.

La plate-forme du pont permet le passage d'une autoroute et d'une voie ferrée entre les deux îles Même si la typologie est maintenue à deux niveaux, les ponts suivent divers modèles comme celui du pont suspendu ou du pont à haubans.

Die Brückenplattform trägt eine Autobahn und eine Schienenverbindung zwischen beiden Inseln. Die Plattform behält ihren Konstruktionstyp auf beiden Ebenen bei, wobei die eigentlichen Brücken im Baustil von einer Hänge- zu einer Schrägseilbrücke wechselt.

Hitsuishijima–Iwakurojima Bridge

Bisan-Seto Bridges

Seto-Ohashi Bridge

Kita & Minami Bisan Seto Bridges

Construction of the Seto-Ohashi Bridge began in 1979 with the the Kita and Minami Bisan-Seto Bridges; it was not until 1988, however, that the six bridges of the Kojima Sakaide Route were completed.

La construction du Seto-Ohashi Bridge débute avec l'élaboration des ponts Kita et Minami Bisan-Seto en 1979. Il faut cependant attendre 1988 pour que les six ponts qui forment la Kojima Sakaide-Route soit achevés.

Der Bau der Seto-Ohashi Bridge begann 1979 mit den Brücken Kita und Minami Bisan-Seto und dauerte bis 1988, als alle sechs Brücken der Kojima Sakaide-Route fertiggestellt wurden.

The Farø Bridges

Monberg & Thorsen A/S
COWI Consultant

FALSTER-FARO, DENMARK. 1980-1985

North bridge length / Longueur du pont nord / Länge der Nordbrücke 1596 m.

South bridge length / Longueur du pont sud / Länge der Südbrücke 1726 m.

Span / Travée / Hauptspannweite 290 m.

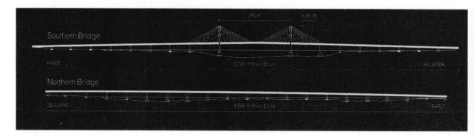

The Farø Bridges, with a total length of 3 322 m., constitute a passageway composed of two bridges which join Zealand with the islands of Faro and Falster. The chosen design is that of the cable-stayed bridge with a metal deck. This deck was one of the most carefully studied elements of the structure. The system which was finally accepted during development of the project involves the use of a metallic casing. This piece would serve for the deck, since it could be divided into numerous prefabricated elements which would later be assembled during construction. This solution would, at the same time, help to resolve other difficulties such as wind problems.

D'une longueur totale de 3 322 m, le Farø Bridges est l'union de deux ponts reliant Zealand, l'île de Faro et l'île de Falster. La typologie sélectionnée ici est celle du pont à haubans avec plateforme métallique. Cette plate-forme a été l'une des pièces les plus étudiées de la structure pendant le développement du projet et une fois celui-ci accepté: une pièce qui, telle une boite métallique, sert de plate-forme permettant la découpe de nombreux éléments préfabriqués pour être ensuite assemblés, et surmontant d'autres problèmes comme celui du vent.

Mit einer Gesamtlänge von 3 322 m, sind The Farø Bridges eine Verbindung zwischen den Inseln Faro und Falster in Seeland, die aus zwei Brücken besteht. Die gewählte Baustruktur in beiden Fällen ist die einer Schrägseilbrücke mit einer metallischen Plattform. Der Plattform wurde bei der Entwicklung des Projekts besondere Aufmerksamkeit gewidmet und am Ende einigte man sich auf das folgende System: die Ebene in Form eines Metallkastens besteht aus vielen vorgefertigten Teilen, die vor Ort zusammengefügt wurden, und so die Lösung für andere Problematiken, wie zum Beispiel den starken Wind in der Region, darstellte.

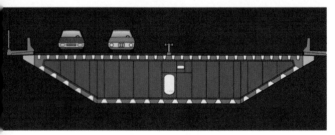

The first proposals for this important pair of bridges already existed by 1979. The south bridge, which leads to the small island of Faro, was the first cable-stayed bridge to be built in Denmark, with a total length of 1 726 m.

Les premières propositions concernant ce grand ensemble de ponts datent de 1979. Le pont sud, qui s'étend jusqu'à la petite île de Faro, a été le premier pont à haubans construit au Danemark. Il mesure 1 726 m de long.

Schon seit 1979 wurden Vorschläge und Projekte zum Bau dieser wichtigen Verbindung ausgearbeitet. Die Südbrücke mit einer Gesamtlänge von 1 726 m ist die erste Schrägseilbrücke, die in Dänemark gebaut wurde.

Kaita Bridge

Hiroshima Prefecture

HIROSHIMA, JAPAN. 1981-1990

Length / Longueur / Gesamtlänge 2350 m.
Span / Travée / Hauptspannweite 250m.

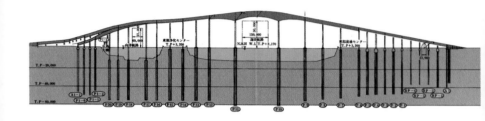

O ne of the consequences of the construction of a bridge is the commercial impulse which such a project may provide. For this reason some construction initiatives are inspired by this necessity. This is the case of the Kaita Bridge, since the work began on this project in 1981 with the explicit intention of promoting the development of the port of Hiroshima, and thus facilitating the transportation and distribution of merchandise in the area. The structural design is simple, based on the idea of a metal deck placed across compound piers. This bridge forms a part of an intricate highway network which belongs to the connection with the Hiroshima-Iwakuni Highway.

U ne des conséquences qui découlent de la construction d'un pont est l'instinct commercial que l'œuvre peut impliquer, et certaines initiatives de construction proviennent de cette nécessité. C'est le cas du Kaita Bridge, où le projet de construction débute en 1981, avec l'intention explicite de promouvoir le développement du port d'Hiroshima et de faciliter le transport et la distribution de marchandises dans la zone. D'un schéma structurel simple basé sur une plate-forme métallique soutenue par des piliers composites, le pont fait partie d'une charpente complexe appartenant à la jonction avec l'autoroute Hiroshima–Iwakuni.

D a der Bau einer Brücke fast immer einen kommerziellen Impuls für die neu zugängliche Region darstellt, werden viele Brücken genau aus diesem Grund gebaut. Einer dieser Fälle ist zum Beispiel die Kaita Bridge, die errichtet wurde um die Entwicklung des Hafens von Hiroshima zu stimulieren und den Transport und die Distribution von Waren in der Gegend zu erleichtern. Im Jahr 1981 begann das Projekt. Mit seiner einfachen Struktur aus einer metallischen Plattform auf mehrteiligen Säulen, bildet diese Brücke Teil der komplexen Zufahrt zur Autobahn Hiroshima–Iwakuni.

黄金山　　猿猴川　　東部浄化センター　　広島大橋　　海田大橋　　東部流通センター

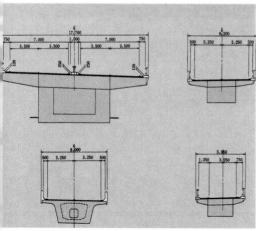

Construction of this bridge, designed according to the Port of Hiroshima Plan, began in 1983 and ended in 1990. It forms a part of the South Hiroshima Highway which leads to the Hiroshima-Iwakuni Highway.

Conçu suivant le Plan du Port d'Hiroshima, les travaux pour ce pont débutent en 1983 et durent jusqu'en 1990. Il fait partie de la route sud d'Hiroshima qui rejoint l'autoroute de Hiroshima-Iwakuni.

Die Bauarbeiten zur Brücke, die designtechnisch im Einklang mit der Planung des Hafens von Hiroshima steht, begannen 1983 und wurden 1990 fertiggestellt. Sie ist Teil einer Straße südlich von Hiroshima, welche zur Autobahn Hiroshima-Iwakuni führt.

The creation of a "Technical Planning Committee" was necessary due to strong determining factors in the region. Thus a structural system using a metal deck was chosen for this, the longest bridge of its typology in Japan.

Dû aux conditions physiques de ce lieu, la création d'un «Comité de Planification Technique» est nécessaire. Le choix de la structure se porte sur un système de plate-forme métallique, pour le pont le plus long du Japon dans cette catégorie.

Wegen der rauhen Bedingungen des Standortes war es notwendig, ein «Komitee zur technischen Planung» zu gründen. So entschied man sich für die Struktur der Metallplattform. Die Brücke ist die längste dieses Konstruktionstyps in Japan.

Puente peatonal sobre el Río Segre

Enric Miralles, Carme Pinos, arq.
E. Prats, arq.; Brufau-Obiols, est.

LLEIDA, ESPAÑA. 1985-1986

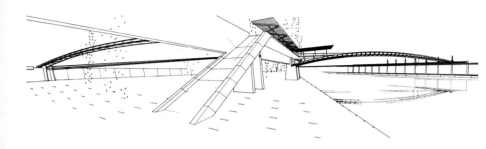

This was one of the projects selected in the 1986 competition announced for the design of a pedestrian bridge over the Segre River as it passes through the historic centre of the city of Lerida. The winning bid in this competition was the one proposed by the architects Mamen Domingo and Ernest Ferré who are also included in this monograph. The proposal by the team composed of Miralles/Pinos and Brufau/Obiols, is that of a footbridge encompassing three linear elements flowing in different directions of pedestrian traffic. One of the most noble and attractive spaces of the project is created at the point where the three "lines" meet.

Ce projet est sélectionné en 1986 lors d'un concours portant sur la conception d'une passerelle pour piétons sur le fleuve Segre en direction du centre historique de la ville de Lérida ; le premier prix est remporté par le projet des architectes Mamen Domingo et Ernest Ferré, également inclus dans cet ouvrage. La proposition de l'équipe Miralles/Pinos et Brufau/Obiols est celle d'une passerelle composée de trois éléments linéaires réunissant les différentes directions du trafic piétonnier; au point de convergence de ces trois «lignes» se trouve un des espaces les plus élégants et fascinants du projet.

Dieser Entwurf war einer der ausgewählten im Zuge des 1986 durchgeführten Wettbewerbs um das Design einer Fußgängerbrücke über den Segre im historischen Stadtkern der Stadt Lerida, den am Ende das Projekt der Architekten Mamen Domingo und Ernest Ferré gewannen (auch in dieser Sammlung berücksichtigt). Das Modell des Teams Miralles/Pinos und Brufau/Obiols schlägt drei lineare Elemente vor, die verschiedene Richtungen des Fußgängerstroms beherbergen und sich am Ende vereinen. An dem Punkt, wo die drei «Linien» zusammenkommen, entsteht der attraktivste und nobelste Teil des Projekts.

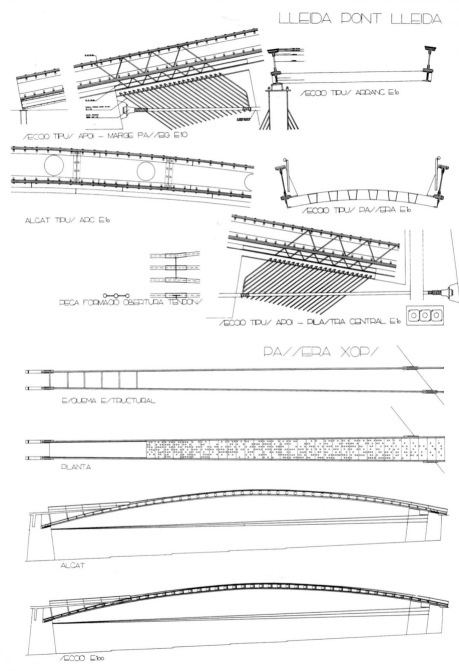

LLEIDA PONT LLEIDA

SECCIO TIPUS ARRANC E16

SECCIO TIPUS APOI - MARGE PASSEG E10

ALCAT TIPUS ARC E16

SECCIO TIPUS PASSERA E16

PEÇA FORMACIO OBERTURA TENDONS

SECCIO TIPUS APOI - PILASTRA CENTRAL E16

PASSERA XOPS

ESQUEMA ESTRUCTURAL

PLANTA

ALCAT

SECCIO E100

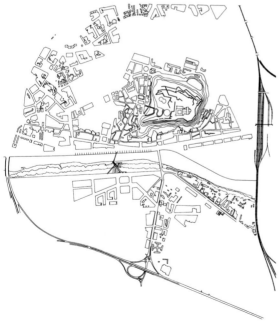

The proposed plan involving three linear elements collects different directions of pedestrian traffic together and channels them into a single direction. In the elevation these three lines become subtle curves passing over the Segre River.

Cette idée de trois éléments linéaires a permis de réunir différentes directions de la circulation piétonnière, qui finissent par confluer en une seule. Au point d'élévation, ces trois lignes se transforment en de fluides passages incurvés sur le fleuve Segre.

Dieses Modell schlägt vor, 3 lineare Elemente für die verschiedenen Richtungen des Fußgängerstroms zu bauen, die dann in eines zusammenfließen. Im Aufriss verwandeln sich diese drei Linien in schmale Wege über den Fluss Segre.

Pasarela Sobre el Río Segre

Mamen Domingo, Ernest Ferré; arq.
A. Aparicio, M. Reventós, ing.
C. Cabré, F. Corada, M. Reventós; arq.

LLEIDA, ESPAÑA. 1986, 1994-1998

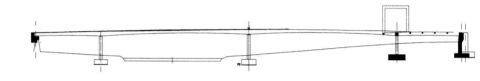

This project, winner of a 1986 competition, is located between the Avenida de Madrid (Madrid Avenue) and Plaza Blas Infante (Blas Infante Square) in the historic centre of Llerida. This footbridge was proposed as a continuation of Cavallers Street, one of the most characteristic streets in the area. In this manner the bridge becomes an inhabited street, where the wooden benches are transformed into living spaces framed by streetlamps. The feel of a dwelling place is reinforced by the manner in which these spaces are "fitted" onto the deck thus increasing the width of the deck to 10 m. At the opposite end of the footbridge we find the elevated square which provides access to Segre Park.

Ce projet, qui remporte un concours en 1986, est construit entre l'Avenue de Madrid et la Place Blas Infante dans le centre historique de Llérida. L'idée de la passerelle est de prolonger la rue Cavallers, une des plus typiques de la zone. Le passage devient une rue où les bancs de bois entourés de réverbères constituent les espaces de détente. Ces espaces «encastrés» sur la plate-forme s'étendent jusqu'à 10 m, accentuant l'idée de station de repos à l'intérieur du pont. De l'autre côté de la passerelle se trouve une place suspendue qui permet l'accès au parc du Segre.

Dieses Projekt gewann den Wettbewerb des Jahres 1986 und befindet sich heute zwischen der Avenida de Madrid und dem Plaza Blas Infante im historischen Zentrum der Stadt Lleida in Spanien. Sie ist die Verlängerung der Straße Cavallers, eine der charakteristischsten der Gegend. So verwandelt sich der Weg in eine lebendige Straße, wo die von Laternen gerahmten Holzbänke und ihre Umgebung zu Orten der Entspannung werden, die so in die Plattform «eingebaut» sind, dass sie eine Breite von bis zu 10 Metern erzielen. Am anderen Ende der Brücke befindet sich ein Platz über, den man zum Ufer und zum Park des Segre gelangt.

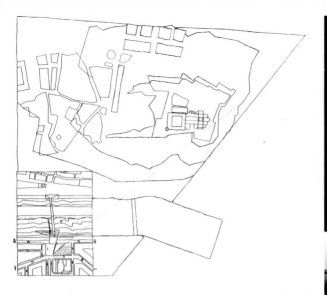

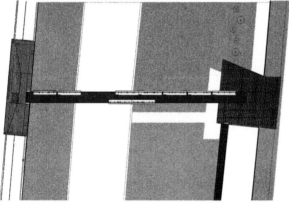

We approach the bridge from the linear Segre Park by means of a cobblestoned ramp which ends at the great elevated square. As a point of reference we find, on this shore, the metallic "Segre River Gate".

On peut accéder à cette passerelle depuis le parc linéaire du Segre au moyen d'une rampe pavée qui donne sur la grande place suspendue. De cette berge, on peut observer comme point de référence la structure métallique de la «Puerta del Segre».

Vom Park des Segre aus gelangt man über eine gepflasterte Rampe, die auf dem Brückenplatz endet, zur Überführung. Von diesem Ufer aus treffen wir auch auf die Metallstruktur «Tor des Segre».

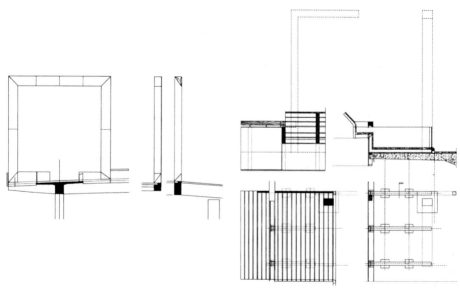

The lighting elements in the bench area were specifically designed for this project: they carry out the function of beacon lighting while at the same time masquerading as armrests. The vertical upright marks the "entrance" to the rest area.

Les éclairages dans la zone des bancs ont été conçus spécialement pour ce projet : en plus de servir d'accoudoir, ils occupent la fonction de balisage lumineux. Le mât vertical marque l'«entrée» dans les zones de détente..

Die Beleuchtungselemente an diesen Bänken wurden extra für dieses Projekt entworfen: sie dienen als Armlehne und gleichzeitig beleuchten sie die Wegmarkierungen. Der vertikale Mast signalisiert den Eingang zur der Zone, die zu einer Pause einlädt.

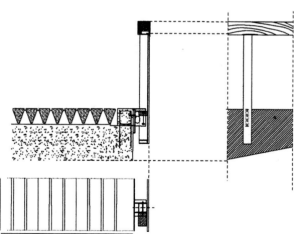

The bench area includes elements which are clearly identifiable on the deck: a widening of the pathway, the use of iroko wood and the position of the streetlamps surrounding and highlighting this area.

Les bancs sont facilement reconnaissables sur la plate-forme : l'élargissement du chemin, l'utilisation de bois d'iroko et la présence des réverbères à leur niveau les mettent en évidence

Die Bänke sind herausragende Elemente auf der Plattform: die Verbreiterung der Wege, die Verwendung von Irokoholz und die Stellung der Laternen heben sie besonders hervor.

The trapezoidal square of 30 x 40 m., like the deck, is made of brown-coloured asphalt. Its structure of concrete slats allows the natural light to pass through, thus creating an attractive shady area beneath the square.

La place trapézoïdale de 30 x 40 m dispose, tout comme la plate-forme, d'un revêtement en asphalte de couleur marron. En forme de lames, sa structure de béton laisse passer la lumière, créant ainsi un bel espace ombragé sous la place.

Der 30 x 40 m große trapezförmige Platz ist genau wie die Plattform braun asphaltiert. Seine Struktur aus Betonplatten lässt nur ein wenig Licht durchfallen, was unterhalb des Platzes einen attraktiven, schattigen Ort entstehen lässt.

Puente Bac de Roda, Felipe II

Santiago Calatrava, arq.

BARCELONA, ESPAÑA. 1985-1987

Length / Longueur / Gesamtlänge 129 m.
Span / Travée / Hauptspannweite 46 m.

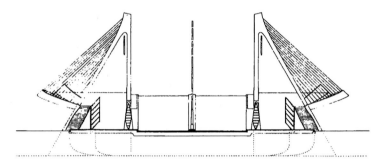

The necessity of joining two areas of the city which had become separated was one of the factors which provided the impetus for the construction of this bridge. A passageway for cars was required, of course, but also one for pedestrians. For this reason, two pairs of structural arches were proposed, which would sustain a car deck flanked by two pedestrian paths. A widening of the area in the centre of these pedestrian paths creates a resting space in the form of look-outs which are, in addition, accentuated by the lighting. In this project we can recognize the characteristic structural studies of the architect, which provide the aesthetics for the project.

Parmi diverses raisons, ce pont est né de la nécessité de réunir deux quartiers de la ville jusqu'alors séparés. Il fallait un pont qui puisse accueillir voitures comme piétons. D'où l'idée de créer deux arcs structuraux supportant une plate-forme pour voitures, longée par deux passages piétonniers, au centre desquels se trouve un élargissement d'où l'on peut admirer la vue grâce à des belvédères mis en valeur par l'éclairage. On reconnaît dans cette œuvre l'étude structurale caractéristique de l'auteur, qui communique l'esthétique de ses projets.

Diese Brücke entstand aus der Notwendigkeit heraus zwei Teile eine Stadt zu vereinen. Man benötig te einen Übergang für Autos aber auch für Fußgänger. So wurden zwei Bogenpaare ge baut, die eine Plattform für der Verkehr stützen und ergänzte diese an den Seiten mi Gehwegen. Im Zentrum diese Gehwege wurden Aussichts punkte geschaffen, an dener sich der Weg verbreitert und die außerdem durch eine besonde re Beleuchtung hervorgehober werden. Bei diesem Projek sind die charakteristischen Strukturstudien des Designers die seinen Werken eine beson dere Ästhetik geben, besonders gut deutlich.

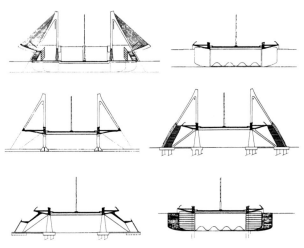

Each pair of arches opens up in the centre to create a pedestrian lane. This opening is used to create a resting space within the pedestrian lane beneath the arch.

Les arcs s'ouvrent par paire dans la partie centrale pour faire place au passage piéton, encadrant ainsi l'élargissement qui se trouve sous ces arcs, et donnant naissance à l'espace de repos à l'intérieur de ce même passage.

Jedes Bogenpaar öffnet sich in seinem Zentrum und verbreitert den Weg um den Fußgängern Durchlass zu gewähren. Die Bögen strecken sich wie ein Dach über diese Wegverbreiterung, die zu einer kurzen Rast einladen, und geben ihnen dadurch einen besonderen Charakter.

162

The use of lighting in this project dramatizes all the more the presence of the look-outs, thus these elements become the undisputed protagonists, clearly perceptible both to users of the bridge as well as to passers-by.

L'éclairage du pont dramatise encore plus la présence de belvédères, donnant à ces éléments le rôle principal, perceptible tant par les utilisateurs du pont que par de simples spectateurs.

Die Beleuchtung des Projekts betont zusätzlich die Existenz der Aussichtspunkte. Diese Elemente übernehmen zweifelsohne die Hauptrolle bei diesem Bau, unabhängig davon ob man die Brücke benutzt oder sie nur von Weitem sieht.

Alex Fraser Bridge

CBA; Buckland & Taylor Ltd.

VANCOUVER-BC, CANADA. 1986

Length / Longueur / Gesamtlänge 930 m.
Span / Travée / Hauptspannweite 465 m.

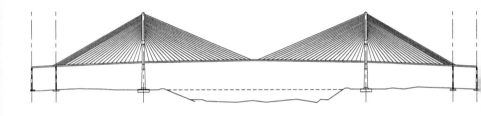

U pon its inauguration, this bridge over the Fraser River became a point of reference for other projects on account of the different technological innovations presented in its design. Even today it continues to be one of the longest cable-stayed bridges in North America. Its simplicity and elegance are based on the careful design of its modular components. This along with a detailed study of its joints and its particular assembly system, permitted the construction process to comply strictly with its timetable while avoiding setbacks. It was therefore possible to inaugurate this bridge after only 31 months of work.

Q uand le pont sur la rivière Fraser est inauguré, il devient un point de référence pour d'autres projets, dû aux innovations technologiques que sa conception comporte; c'est aujourd'hui encore l'un des ponts à haubans les plus grands d'Amérique. Sa simplicité et son élégance sont fondées sur une conception soignée des éléments modulaires, qui, en plus de l'étude détaillée des jointures et de son système d'assemblage, ont permis sa construction

A ls man diese Brücke über dem Fluss Fraser einweihte, wurde sie durch ihre technologischen Neuerungen im Design zum Vorbild für zahlreiche spätere Projekte. Noch heutzutage ist sie eine der längsten Schrägseilbrücken Amerikas. Ihre einfache Eleganz basiert auf dem sorgfältigen Design seiner bausteinartigen Einzelteile, die durch ein bis ins äußerste Detail studiertes System unter Einhaltung aller Zeitpläne sehr schnell zusammengefügt wurden. Schon nach 31 Monaten Bauzeit wurde die Brücke fertiggestellt.

The careful attention to detail on this bridge assured that not even the elements most imperceptible to the public eye would be overlooked. This is demonstrated by the joints between the cables and the pylons and their anchorage to the ground.

Dans l'étude minutieuse des détails qui constituent ce pont, rien n'a été laissé de côté, pas même les éléments les moins perceptibles pour l'utilisateur, comme le démontrent les jointures entre les traverses et la tour, ou encore son ancrage au sol.

Das sorgfältige Studium aller Details dieser Brücke hat auch die für den Benutzer kaum sichtbaren Elemente nicht außer Acht gelassen, was die Befestigungen der Seile an den Türmen oder ihre Verankerungen im Boden beweisen.

The Askoy Bridge

Bridge Department of the Directorate of Public Roads.

Aas-Jakobsen, ing.; Monberg & Thorsen A/S

BERGEN, NORWAY. 1987-1992

Length / Longueur / Gesamtlänge 1057 m.
Span / Travée / Hauptspannweite 850 m.

A n examination of a possible connection to the island of Askoy, located near Bergen, was already underway since 1960. Nonetheless this suspension bridge, the longest in Norway, was not inaugurated until 1992. The projected deck provides passage for two car lanes and one pedestrian path and was designed allowing for the possibility of an addition, since it currently supports a heavy flow of traffic. This addition could provide a total of three car lanes and two pedestrian paths. Its structure combines concrete with prefabricated metal pieces. The execution of this project involved the use of innovative systems of construction management.

L es études sur une connexion avec l'île d'Askoy, près de Bergen, remontent à 1960, mais ce n'est qu'en 1992 que ce pont suspendu, le plus long de toute la Norvège, est inauguré. Sa plate-forme comprend deux voies pour les voitures et un passage piéton. Ce pont a été élaboré en prenant en compte l'éventualité d'un agrandissement : devant actuellement supporter une importante circulation routière, il pourrait, une fois agrandi, totaliser trois voies de voitures et deux passages piétonniers. Sa structure associe béton et pièces métalliques préfabriquées. Des systèmes de mise en œuvre novateurs ont été utilisés pour mener à bien l'exécution de ce projet.

S chon seit 1960 wurde eine Verbindung mit der Insel Askoy in der Nähe von Bergen in Betracht gezogen. Allerdings dauerte es bis 1992, als endlich die längste Hängebrücke Norwegens eingeweiht werden konnte. Die Plattform wurde mit 2 Fahrspuren für Autos und einem Gehweg versehen, wobei man sich bei ihrem Bau die Möglichkeit einer Erweiterung offen hielt und die Brücke bald über eine weitere Fahrspur und zwei zusätzliche Gehwege verfügen könnte. Ihre Struktur kombiniert Beton und vorgefertigte Metallteile. Bei der Durchführung dieses Projekts kamen neue Systeme des Brückenbaus zum Einsatz.

The work was carried out in four steps: two cables were mounted by means of the construction of two "footbridges" which followed the path of the main cables. The prefabricated pieces were then suspended from these cables and moved from there to their final positions.

Les travaux ont été répartis en quatre étapes : grâce à la construction de deux «passerelles» suivant la direction des câbles principaux, on a pu monter les deux câbles puis accrocher les éléments préfabriqués, ensuite transférés jusqu'à leur position adéquate.

Die Bauarbeiten wurden in vier Phasen geteilt: nachdem zwei provisorische «Übergänge» gefertigt wurden, die dem Verlauf der zuerst gespannten Kabel entsprach, montierte man zwei weitere Kabel, an die die vorgefertigten Teile gehängt und danach montiert wurden.

The height of the towers, 152 m., prevented the crane barges from positioning the prefabricated pieces on the deck. For this reason a special system called telegraphing was developed in order to place these elements in their final locations.

La hauteur des tours, 152 mètres, ne permettait pas aux grues de poser les pièces préfabriquées de la plate-forme à leur place. Un système spécial, le telegraphing, a donc été développé pour pouvoir les amener jusqu'à leur position finale.

Die Höhe der Türme, 152 Meter, machte es für die Schwimmkräne unmöglich die vorgefertigten Teile an ihrem Platz auf der Plattform anzubringen. Darum musste ein neues System entwickelt werden –Telegraphing– um diese an den für sie vorgesehen Ort zu montieren.

181

Thames Court Footbridge

Whitby Bird & Partners

LONDON, UNITED KINGDOM. 1987

Length / Longueur / Gesamtlänge 57,7 m.
Span / Travée / Hauptspannweite 25,5 m.

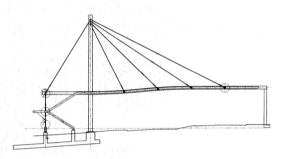

This project, located on Upper Thames Street, was developed following an exhaustive study of the pedestrian traffic in the area and an analysis of the visual impact of the new bridge. Another important factor in the design was the necessity of placing a minimum number of supports on the north shore as well as the control of the visual effect which would be created from Wren Church in the east. The solution which was finally chosen was that of a cable-stayed structure, where the deck would be supported by a cantilever with a pipe suspended from the single upright of the bridge. The simplicity of the project required a detailed study of each of its constructive elements.

Situé dans la rue Upper Thames Street, ce projet est le résultat d'une étude approfondie du trafic piétonnier dans cette zone, suivie d'une analyse de l'impact visuel du nouveau pont. Un autre facteur important dans la conception de cette passerelle est la nécessité d'inclure le moins de supports possibles du côté nord, en plus de contrôler l'angle de vision à partir de l'église Wren, à l'est. On est donc parvenu à la solution d'une structure à haubans où la plate-forme est soutenue en porte-à-faux par un tube suspendu à l'unique mât du pont. La simplicité de ce projet permet une étude minutieuse de chacun de ses éléments constructifs.

Dieses Projekt wurde einer ausgiebigen Studie der Fußgängerströme und einer Analyse des visuellen Impakts der neuen Brücke zu Folge entwickelt und befindet sich in der Upper Thames Street. Zwei weitere wichtige Faktoren beim Design dieser Brücke waren einerseits die Notwendigkeit, an der Nordseite so wenig wie möglich Verankerungen anzubringen, andererseits die Aussicht auf die Brücke von der Kirche Wren im östlichen Teil. So kam man zu der Lösung einer Schrägseilstruktur, bei der sich die Plattform im Cantilever auf ein Rohr stützt, das vom einzigen Mast der Brücke abhängt. Die Einfachheit der Brücke ist auf ein sorgfältiges Studium jedes einzelnen Bauelements zurückzuführen.

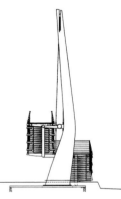

The pipe suspended from the upright is one of the main components of the structure: the entire deck is supported by a cantilever which permits a connection to this new roadway from Upper Thames Street.

Le segment tubulaire suspendu au mât constitue l'un des éléments principaux de la structure : c'est sur lui que repose la plateforme entière de passage, qui permet la connexion avec l'artère Upper Thames Street.

Das Rohr, das vom einzigen Mast der Brücke abhängt, ist eines der Hauptteile der Struktur: von ihm aus wird im Cantilever die die gesamte Plattform unterstützt, die Verknüpfung dieser neuen Arterie in der Upper Thames Street ermöglicht.

Fußgangerbrücke über Neckar

Schlaich Bergermann und Partner, ing.
Brigitte Schlaich-Peterhans, arq.

STUTTGART, DEUTSCHLAND. 1988

Length and Span / Longueur eTravée / Gesamtlänge ?? Hauptspannweite114 m.

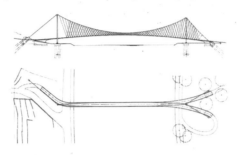

This footbridge over the Neckar River was planned near Max-Eyth-See in Stuttgart, in a quiet natural scenic area. A sloping hillside on one shore and a flat park on the other made it necessary to search for a structure capable of adapting itself to both shores. For this reason and following numerous studies, the suspension bridge was the model chosen for this passage. After construction of the pylons and installation of the main cable from which the secundary cables were run, a prefabricated concrete deck was installed from the centre. This deck was then completed on each side by placing the remaining modular pieces in position.

Près de Max–Eyth–See à Stuttgart, dans un paisible site naturel, cette passerelle enjambe le fleuve Neckar. D'un côté, on peut apercevoir une colline escarpée, et de l'autre, un parc au relief plat, d'où la nécessité de trouver une structure pouvant s'adapter aux deux rives à la fois. Ainsi, après de nombreuses recherches, c'est le modèle du pont suspendu qui est sélectionné. Avant la construction des tours et l'installation du câble principal auquel est relié un groupe de câbles secondaires, on installe une plateforme préfabriquée en béton qui va du centre à chacun des côtés au moyen d'éléments modulaires.

Dieser Übergang des Neckar befindet sich in einer ruhigen Naturzone in der Nähe des Max–Eyth–Sees in Stuttgart. Ein Hügel auf einer Seite und ein flacher Park auf der anderen machten es notwendig eine Struktur zu finden, die sich an die Gegebenheiten beider Ufer anpasst. Als Ergebnis diverser Studien wurde eine Hänge-brücke als Lösung gewählt. Nach der Errichtung der Türme und der Installation des Hauptkabels, von dem aus eine Gruppe von Sekundärkabeln ausgeht, wurde, vom Zentrum her beginnend, eine vorgefertigte Betonplattform in beide Richtungen durch Zusammensetzen der Bausteine angebracht.

187

Thanks to the careful design of each one of its elements, this suspension bridge gives an image of tremendous lightness and delicacy in its structure, adapting itself perfectly to the natural landscape without causing a strong impact while at the same time overcoming the imposed obstacle.

Ce pont suspendu donne une image de légèreté et de finesse structurelle, grâce à une conception élaborée de chacun de ses éléments, et parvient à surmonter l'obstacle imposé sans choquer, mais en s'adaptant au paysage naturel.

Diese Hängebrücke vermittelt dank des sorgfältigen Designs jedes einzelnen Elements ein Bild von Leichtigkeit und Eleganz, passt sich ihrer natürlichen Umgebung an ohne einen großen Impakt in ihr zu bewirken und erfüllt doch bestens seine Funktion.

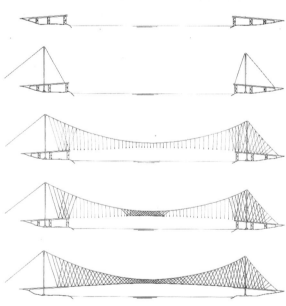

The versatility of the structural typology used allows this project to adapt itself to both placement situations: on one shore it glides gently into the sloping vineyard and on the other it rests upon the plains of the park.

Grâce à la variété de sa typologie structurale, ce pont s'adapte à toutes les conditions du site : d'un côté, il s'ouvre sur la colline escarpée de vignobles, et de l'autre, il se pose au-dessus de la plaine qui constitue le parc.

Durch die Wandlungsfähigkeit des angewendeten Konstruktionstyps passt sich die Brücke den unterschiedlichen Gegebenheiten der beiden Ufer an: auf einer Seite mündet sie in einen Weinberg und auf der anderen posiert sie über der Ebene des Parks.

Puente La Barqueta

Juan Arenas, Marcos Pantaleón ing.
Auxidesa
SEVILLA, ESPAÑA. 1988-1989
Length / Longueur / Gesamtlänge 170 m.

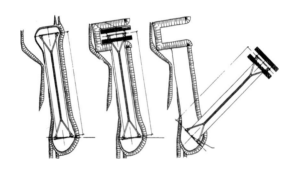

T he issues raised in a city crossed by a river must be closely related to the subject of bridges. This physical condition generates a great variety of virtues: the urban roadways become enriched, the architecture takes on new patterns and the city as a whole must adapt itself to its special conditions. This is the situation of Seville which is crossed by the Guadalquivir River, hence the construction of bridges is of vital importance for its functioning. Thus this bridge is one of those in charge of joining the historic centre with the island of La Cartuja by means of a metallic structure based on the arch.

L' idée d'une ville traversée par un fleuve est étroitement liée à la thématique du pont. Cette situation géographique ouvre des possibilités de diverse nature : les voies urbaines se développent, l'architecture acquiert de nouveaux thèmes et la ville doit s'adapter à sa condition particulière. C'est le cas de Séville, traversée par le fleuve Guadalquivir, et où la construction de ponts est essentielle à son fonctionnement. Ainsi, ce pont a la fonction de relier le centre historique et l'île de La Cartuja, au moyen d'une structure métallique basée sur le modèle de l'arc.

D ie Planung einer Stadt die von einem Fluss durchquert wird, ist unweigerlich an das Thema Brücken gebunden. Von diesem physischen Umstand ausgehend kann der Charakter einer Stadt sehr beeinflusst werden: die städtischen Wege werden bereichert und die Architektur nimmt neue Themen auf, da sich die Stadt ihren Gegebenheiten anpassen muss. Das ist der Fall beim Beispiel der Stadt Sevilla, die vom dem Fluss Guadalquivir durchquert wird, und somit der Brückenbau vital für ihre Funktionstüchtigkeit ist. Diese Brücke hat es zur Aufgabe, das historische Zentrum über eine auf einem Bogen basierte Metallstruktur mit der Insel La Cartuja zu verbinden.

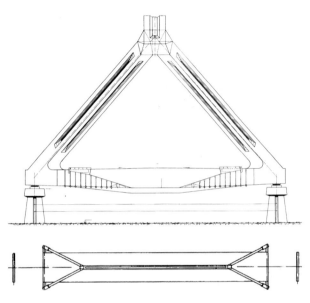

The La Barqueta Bridge stands out for the simplicity of its lines, which lends it great transparency on a formal level. This is due largely to the fact that only one group of supporting cables running out from the arch exists, which avoids any sort of visual interference.

La simplicité de ses lignes donne une grande transparence des formes au pont de La Barqueta. Ceci est en grande partie dû au fait qu'il n'y a qu'un seul groupe de tenseurs qui sort de l'arc, ce qui permet d'éviter les interférences visuelles.

Die Brücke La Barqueta fällt vor allem durch die Einfachheit ihrer Linien auf, die ihrer Gesamterscheinung eine große Transparenz verleiht. Das wurde vor allem durch die Anbringung nur einer Gruppe von Spannern am Bogen erreicht, was visuelle Interferenzen vermeidet.

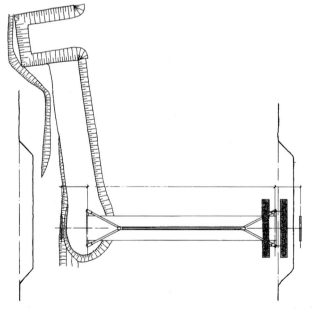

At the point where it meets the ground, the arch divides into two in order to form a pair of pillars. Although the fundamental reasons for this are structural, on a formal level this design is also used to frame the approach to the bridge.

Au point de rencontre avec le sol, l'arc se divise en deux pour faire place à deux piliers. Bien que sa raison fondamentale soit sa structure, les formes de cette œuvre sont également exploitées afin de faire ressortir les accès au pont.

Bevor er den Boden berührt, teilt sich der Bogen in zwei Säulen. Der Grund dafür ist hauptsächlich struktureller Natur, wobei die Säulen dadurch auch optisch die Funktion der Zugangsmarkierung zur Brücke erfüllen.

The bridge was originally planned as a footbridge at the start of the project, but during the process the necessities changed. It was therefore transformed into a path for both pedestrians and vehicles, which increased the scale of the structure.

Au début du projet, le pont est destiné uniquement aux piétons, mais au cours de la construction, les besoins évoluent et il se transforme en un passage fréquenté par piétons et voitures, ce qui donne une nouvelle dimension à sa structure.

Zu Beginn des Projekts war eine reine Fußgängerbrücke geplant, aber im Laufe der Vorbereitungen wurde die Notwendigkeit eines Übergangs für Fußgänger und Fahrzeuge immer deutlicher, was das Projekt bedeutend bereicherte.

Puente Lusitania

Santiago Calatrava, arq.

MÉRIDA, ESPAÑA. 1988-1991

Longitud / Lunghezza / Longitude 465 m.
Span / Travée / Hauptspannweite 189 m.

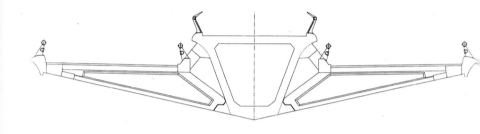

Since Roman times a passageway over the Guadiana River was of prime importance to the city of Merida. As witness to this fact we find the remains of the famous Roman bridge. However, as in a large number of cases, the expansion of the city made the existing bridges insufficient. In consequence, the Government of Extremadura decided to encourage the projection of a new bridge over the river. This new passageway was created with a continuous deck separated into three parts: in the centre, formally highlighted by the arch, we find the elevated pedestrian path. On both sides in cantilever the two car lanes enjoy an exceptional view over the river.

Depuis l'époque de la Rome antique, un passage sur le fleuve Guardiana était un besoin essentiel dans la ville de Mérida ; on peut citer les vestiges du fameux pont romain. Mais comme c'est souvent le cas, les passages existants ne suffisent plus à subvenir aux besoins de la ville en expansion. La Junta de Extremadura décide donc de lancer le projet d'un nouveau pont sur la rivière, constitué d'une plateforme continue mais divisée en trois. Au centre se trouve un passage surélevé pour les piétons, mis en évidence par un arc et entouré de deux voies pour les voitures avec une vue privilégiée sur la rivière.

Schon im römischen Zeitalter war die Brücke über den Fluss Guadiana in der Stadt Merida unverzichtbar geworden, was die noch immer existierende römische Brücke beweist. Aber wie in vielen Fällen reichen die vorhandenen Übergänge durch das starke Städtewachstum nicht mehr aus. Also beschloss das Land Extremadura das Projekt einer neuen Brücke über den Fluss ins Leben zu rufen. Die neue Brücke besteht aus einer durchgängigen dreifach längsgeteilten Plattform: in der Mitte befindet sich der erhöhte Gehweg, der vom Brückenbogen überdacht wird, und an der Seiten die Fahrbahnen für Autos, von denen aus man eine besonders schöne Aussicht über den Fluss hat.

The arch located on the centre axis of the bridge highlights the pedestrian path in a formal manner above the car lanes. This fact also serves to resolve a functional question: its elevation provides it with a natural separation from the car lanes.

L'arc situé sur l'axe central du pont permet de faire ressortir le passage piéton au-dessus de la chaussée, ce qui constitue également une solution à niveau fonctionnel : la situation surélevée du passage piétons assure une séparation naturelle avec la voie réservée aux voitures.

Der Bogen, der sich auf der Zentralachse der Brücke befindet, macht den Gehweg visuell auffälliger als die Fahrbahnen. Durch die Erhöhung des Streifens für Fußgänger, erzielte man auch eine funktionelle Trennung der drei Teile der Plattform.

Neue Werrabrucke

PPL Planungsgruppe Professor Laage, Prof. H.G. Burkhardt
Erikson, Meyer + Partner; Engineering
HANNOVERSCH-MÜNDEN, DEUTSCHLAND. 1988-1994

Length / Longueur / Gesamtlänge 95 m.
Span / Travée / Hauptspannweite 65 m.

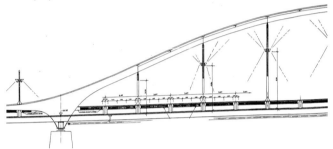

The region of Lower Saxony over the Werra River is the setting for this project. This bridge, based upon the design of a pair of metal arches and a combined concrete deck, forms a part of the new Hannover Münden highway network; its aim is to resolve the question of the heavy traffic flow from this city. The deck is sustained by a group of metal cables suspended from the two arches. Both cables and arches are made of the same material which permits the joints to be designed in an optimum fashion. Where the cables meet the deck, they act as a functional, formal barrier between car lanes and pedestrian paths.

Cette jonction est située sur le Werra, dans la basse Saxe. Constitué de deux arcs métalliques et d'une plate-forme combinée de béton, ce pont fait partie du nouveau réseau routier de Hannover Münden, dont l'objectif est la décongestion du trafic routier de la ville. La plate-forme est supportée par un groupe de traverses métalliques qui relie les deux arcs. Traverses et arcs sont fabriqués à partir du même matériel, ce qui constitue une solution optimale par rapport aux jointures. Les traverses, à leur point de rencontre avec la plate-forme, agissent telle une barrière fonctionnelle et formelle entre les voies automobiles et piétonnes.

Das Land Niedersachse ist Schauplatz diese Brücke über die Werra Sie besteht aus zw Metallbögen und einer komb nierten Betonplattform un ist Teil des neuen Straßenne zes Hannover Münden, da das Problem des starke Verkehrsaufkommens in de Stadt lösen soll. Die Plattfor wird von einer Gruppe vo Stahlseilen, die an den Böge angebracht sind, gehalten. D Seile und die Bögen sind au dem gleichen Material, wa deren Verbindung und Befes gung erleichtert. Weiterhin ste len die Träger eine Barriere zw schen den Fahrbahnen f Autos und den Gehwegen f Fußgänger dar.

The fluidity in the design of the arch and its location within the project highlight even further the sensation upon entering and leaving the bridge. Hence, the pair of arches act as "access gates" to the bridge.

La fluidité dans l'approche de l'arc et son emplacement à l'intérieur du projet accentuent la sensation d'entrée et de sortie du pont. Les deux arcs jouent le rôle des «portes» d'accès au pont.

Die Bögen verstärken durch die Flüssigkeit ihres Designs und ihre Stellung innerhalb des Projekts das Gefühl des Hereinfahrens und Verlassens der Brücke. Sie vermitteln den Anschein, die «Tore» zur Brücke darzustellen.

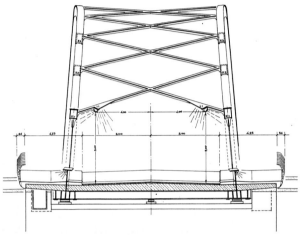

The two metal arches act as one unit: the pieces which join them convert them into one sole element in both a formal and a structural manner. The components required to support the deck were subsequently "suspended" from the pair of arches.

Les deux arcs métalliques fonctionnent comme une même unité : les pièces qui les unissent les transforment en un élément unique tant du point de vue formel que structurel. Les éléments nécessaires «s'accrochent» ensuite à ces deux arcs pour soutenir la plateforme.

Die zwei Metallbögen fungieren als eine Einheit: die Teile, die sie verbinden, verwandeln sie in ein einziges Element sowie form- als auch strukturtechnisch. Beim Bau der Brücke wurden zuerst die Bögen errichtet um danach die benötigten Stahlseile an diese «anzuhängen».

Pasarela junto Plaza Karl Marx

Llorens & Soldevila, arq.
B. de Sola, M.M Sola, I. Lizundia, J.R Vazquez, arq.
BARCELONA, ESPAÑA. 1989

Length / Longueur / Gesamtlänge 42 m.

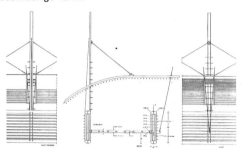

When a bridge or footpath crosses over other roadways, it is important to study the design from all angles including the view "from below". All the viewpoints were carefully projected in this footbridge as can be seen from its lower façade, where we find a complete lack of the closed-in sensation. The use of an H-shaped beam and a meticulous handling of its transparency create a feeling of the lightness of a brief passageway. Once upon this bridge, however, careful control of the visual environment and the height of the railings give a sense of security to this path over the freeway.

Quand une passerelle ou un pont traverse d'autres voies de circulation, il est important d'étudier la conception à tout point de vue, sans oublier la façade «vu d'en bas». Tous les aspects visuels de cette œuvre ont été minutieusement étudiés, comme le montre la façade inférieure, où l'on peut observer l'absence d'une volumétrie fermée. L'utilisation d'une poutre en forme de «H» et le traitement des transparences créent une sensation de légèreté. Pourtant, une fois sur ce pont, le contrôle des angles de vision et la hauteur des balustrades garantissent la sécurité de ce passage au-dessus de l'autoroute.

Wenn Übergänge und Brücken andere Straßen und Wege kreuzen, ist es besonders wichtig deren Design aus allen Sichtpunkten zu studieren, wobei auch die Fassade «von unten» nicht zu vergessen ist. Bei diesem Übergang beschäftigte man sich sorgfältig mit allen möglichen Blickwinkeln, was sein Anblick von unten beweist. Die Anbringung der stützenden Balken in «H-Form» und ihre Lichtdurchlässigkeit vermitteln ein Gefühl der Leichtigkeit. Befindet man sich auf der Brücke hat man aber, vor allem durch das hohe Geländer, trotzdem das Gefühl der Sicherheit und Stabilität.

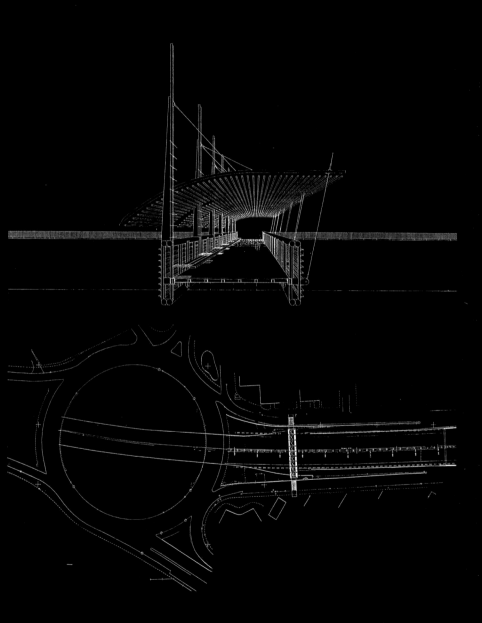

The choice of an H-shaped beam for the deck allows the footbridge to formally appear much lighter. This fact along with a careful handling of the vertical planes, all of which are permeable to the light, strengthen this intention.

Le choix d'une poutre en forme de «H» pour la plate-forme permet une structure de la passerelle beaucoup plus légère. Ce facteur, en plus du traitement de tous les plans verticaux, qui laissent passer la lumière, conforte cette intention.

Die Wahl der stützenden Balken der Plattform in «H–Form» und die Lichtdurchlässigkeit des Baus bewirken eine besonders leichte Erscheinung dieser Fußgängerbrücke.

Shima-Maruyama Bridge

Mitsunori Katoh & Shinichi Kondoh
Prefectura de Mie, Sumitomo Construction

TOKYO, JAPAN. 1989

Length / Longueur / Gesamtlänge 318 m.
Span / Travée / Hauptspannweite 104 m.

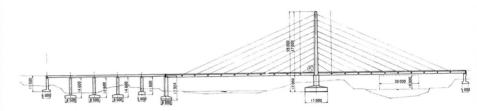

On account of the geographic conditions and the shaky seismic situation, building a bridge in Japan involves the development of detailed structural studies which frequently result in rather complex solutions in the designs. The Shima–Maruyama Bridge, while taking into account the abovementioned factors, is nonetheless an excellent example of a formally simple structure with a delicate attention to detail. Even so, it complied rigourously with the seismic requirements of the region while at the same time introducing constructive processes which had not been used up till the moment.

Dû aux conditions géographique et aux risques de séismes, construire un pont au Japon signifie procéder à une étude structurale détaillée, qui aboutit souvent sur des propositions assez complexes. Néanmoins, le Shima–Maruyama Bridge est un exemple de structure formellement simple aux détails soigneusement étudiés, où aucun de ces facteurs n'a été négligé. Ce pont a été érigé suivant un processus constructif tout nouveau à l'époque, et dans le strict respect des normes sismiques de la zone.

Durch die geografischen und seismischen Umstände Japans ist der Bau einer Brücke in diesem Gebiet oft schwierig und bedarf einer besonders detaillierten Studie. Deshalb sind die Brückenprojekte in Japan oft besonders komplex und kompliziert. Obwohl keiner der lebenswichtigen Punkte außer Acht gelassen wurde, ist die Shima–Maruyama Bridge formtechnisch ein eher einfaches Projekt, bei dem aber jedes Detail einer genauen Analyse unterzogen wurde. Die Brücke erfüllt natürlich die strengen Bestimmungen wegen der seismischen Bewegungen Japans und wurde unter Anwendung eines bis dahin neuen Konstruktionsprozesses errichtet.

This bridge bases its formal image upon one single pylon constructed asymmetrically, from which all the supporting cables which provide structural rigidity to the deck are run. Careful handling of the pylon make it the most characteristic element on the bridge.

L'image formelle de ce pont réside dans sa tour unique, construite asymétriquement et reliée à tous les tenseurs qui donnent sa rigidité structurelle à la plate-forme. La tour, consciencieusement élaborée, en est l'élément le plus caractéristique.

Den Charakter dieser Brücke macht hauptsächlich ihr besonders sorgfältig gepflegter Turm aus, der asymmetrisch angebracht wurde und alle Spanner aufnimmt, die der Struktur ihren Halt geben.

Helgeland Bridge

Knut AAS-Jakobsen; Elljarn Jordet; Sturla K. Rambjor, ing.

Gleitbau Salzburg

HELGELAND, NORWAY. 1989-1991

Length / Longueur / Gesamtlänge 1065 m.
Span / Travée / Hauptspannweite 425 m.

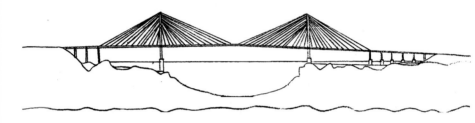

T he very physical structure of countries such as Norway make the presence of bridges a primary factor for guaranteeing proper connections between all the regions of the country. Helgeland Bridge can be found in northern Norway, in an attractive fjord area. Its typology is that of the cable-stayed bridge and is one of the longest in the world. The strong wind currents in the region make constant control of this structure a necessity. For this reason the Public Roads Administration of Norway (PRA), owner of several bridges, developed a special program to monitor the longest structures including that of Helgeland.

D ans les pays comme la Norvège, la structure géographique rend la présence de ponts essentielle pour assurer les connexions entre chaque région. Au nord de la Norvège, dans une ravissante région de fjords, se trouve le pont Helgeland, de type pont à haubans, et faisant partie des plus longs du monde. Les forts vents que l'on trouve à cet endroit obligent le contrôle constant de la structure. Ainsi, l'administration norvégienne des voies publiques (PRA), propriétaire de divers ponts, a développé un programme spécial de surveillance de certains des plus grands ponts, parmi lesquels Helgeland.

I n Ländern wie Norwegen ist die Existenz einer großen Anzahl von Brücken ein absolutes Muss um die Kommunikation und Verbindung aller Regionen des Landes miteinander garantieren zu können. In einer Fjord – Landschaft im Norden Norwegens finden wir die Helgeland Brücke. Ihr Konstruktionstyp entspricht dem einer Schrägseilbrücke, wobei die Helgeland eine der längsten der Welt dieser Bauweise ist. Die starken Winde machen eine ständige Kontrolle der Brücken unabdinglich. Darum hat die Verwaltung öffentlicher Straßen Norwegens (PRA), die einige wichtige Brücken besitzt, ein spezielles Überwachungsprogramm für die längsten Brücken entwickelt, zu denen auch die Helgeland zählt.

The delicate design of the ensemble was planted in the region with utmost care. Its slender concrete pylons support the deck which slips into the landscape as a necessary connecting passageway.

Ce pont au style raffiné est établi dans la région avec le plus grand soin. Ses fines tours de béton soutiennent la plate-forme qui s'intègre au paysage comme une ligne de rattachement nécessaire.

Das dezente Design der Brücke passt sich auf harmonische Weise der Umgebung an. Seine eleganten Betontürme halten die Plattform, die sich wie eine notwendige Verbindungslinie in die Landschaft einfügt.

Pont de Bourgogne

Charles Lavigne, arq.; SETRA: T. Kretz, JM. Lacombe, J. Resplendino, M. Virlogeux

León Grosse; Cabinet Tonello; Sogelerg; A. Chauvin; Freyssinet

CHALON, FRANCE. 1989-1992

Length / Longueur / Gesamtlänge 351 m.
Span / Travée / Hauptspannweite 152 m.

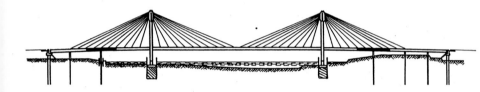

T his bridge over the Saône River was built as the third option to provide a passageway between the cities of Chalon-sur-Saône and Saint-Marcel, since the two bridges already in existence were subjected to intense traffic. The structural design used is that of the cable-stayed bridge combining exposed concrete with steel. The first image which one receives of this bridge is that of its concrete pylons. The deck, made of pre-stressed concrete, provides passage for car lanes and two pedestrian paths. The joints of the galvanized guylines of both the deck and the pylons received special attention.

C e pont, qui traverse la Saône, a été construit comme voie supplémentaire pour permettre le passage entre les villes de Chalon-sur-Saône et Saint-Marcel, car les deux ponts déjà existants étaient soumis à une circulation intense. Le modèle suivi ici est celui du pont à haubans, alliant béton brut et acier. La première image que l'on voit en arrivant sur le pont est celle de ses tours en béton. La plate-forme, en béton précontraint, permet le passage à la fois de voiture et de piétons. Une attention toute particulière a été portée sur les jointures des tenseurs galvanisés, aussi bien pour la plate-forme que pour les tours.

D iese Brücke über dem Fluss Saône war die dritte die zwischen den Städten Chalon-sur-Saône und Sant-Marcel gebaut wurde, da die ersten beiden durch den hohen Verkehr überlastet waren. Die Schrägseilbrücke besteht aus Sichtbeton und Stahl. Ihre Betontürme sind das erste, was beim Überqueren des Flusses ins Auge fällt. Die Plattform aus Spannbeton bietet Platz für eine Straße und 2 Gehwege. Den Befestigungselementen der galvanisierten Spanner, sowohl an der Plattform wie auch an den Türmen, wurde besondere Aufmerksamkeit gewidmet.

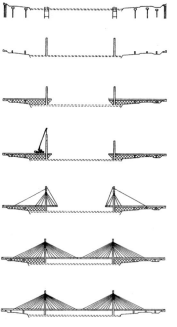

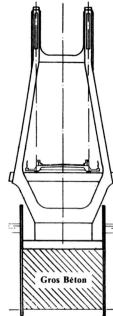

Gros Béton

We can identify the different phases of the construction process of the bridge in its graphic outline, as well as the use of auxiliary elements and structures which were only withdrawn upon completion of the project.

On peut observer dans le schéma de construction du pont les différentes étapes des travaux ainsi que l'emploi d'éléments et de structures auxiliaires, retirées seulement une fois l'œuvre terminée.

Im grafischen Schema des Bauprozesses kann man seine verschiedenen Phasen ausmachen. Es mussten zum Beispiel Hilfsstrukturen errichtet werden, die nach Beendigung der Bauarbeiten wieder entfernt wurden.

The typology chosen for the pylons allows the deck to pass through them. The joints of the guylines to the different elements of the bridge received special attention.

La typologie adoptée ici perme le passage de la plate-forme a travers des tours. Le point d rencontre entre les tenseurs e les autres éléments de l'ensem ble est d'un intérêt tout particu lier au niveau des joints.

Die gewählte Bauweise für di Türme lässt es zu, dass di Plattform durch diese hindurc verläuft. Den Befestigungsele menten der Spanner mit de restlichen Elementen des Pro jekts ist besondere Aufmerk samkeit gewidmet wurden.

Pasarela en la Avda. Meridiana

Llorens & Soldevila, arq.

M.M Sola, I. Lizundia, J.R Vázquez, arq.

BARCELONA, ESPAÑA. 1990

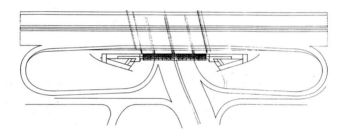

When City Hall commissioned this project, it asked that, in addition to providing a passage for pedestrians between two points, it should also present a façade running parallel to and overlooking Meridiana Avenue. Thus the designers conceived of this footbridge as a genuine overhang facing towards the avenue. A large caisson beam would provide a protected and direct passageway through its interior. Furthermore, two additional levels would be consolidated on top of the beam to create an urban promenade. A group of strands running from the beam would sustain the decks which, along with the pergola, would clearly delimit the different levels of passage.

Lorsque la Commune prend en charge ce projet, c'est avec l'objectif non seulement de créer une liaison piétonne entre deux points, mais également d'établir une façade parallèle à l'Avenida Meridiana. Les créateurs de cette passerelle la considèrent comme une véritable élévation au-dessus de l'avenue. Une grande poutre caisson permet de passer directement à l'intérieur du chemin protégé, et consolide deux niveaux supplémentaires de passage dans le style d'une avenue urbaine. A partir de cette grande poutre part un groupe de cordons reliés aux plates-formes, lesquelles, en plus de la pergola, délimitent nettement les différents niveaux de passage.

Als die Stadt den Bau dieser Brücke plante, beauftragte man die Architekten nicht nur die Verbindung zweier Punkte für Fußgänger zu schaffen, sondern zusätzlich eine parallele Fassade zur Avenida Meridiana zu gestalten. So wurde dieser Übergang von seinen Autoren zu einem wirklichen Aufstieg zur Avenida gemacht. Ein großer geschlossener Träger bietet die Möglichkeit des geschützten und direkten Übergangs durch sein Inneres. Außerdem übernimmt er die Funktion des Stützens zweier weiterer Ebenen, die eher zu einem städtischen Spaziergang einladen. Die Seile zur Halterung der Plattform trennen gemeinsam mit den Masten die verschiedenen Wege über die Brücke.

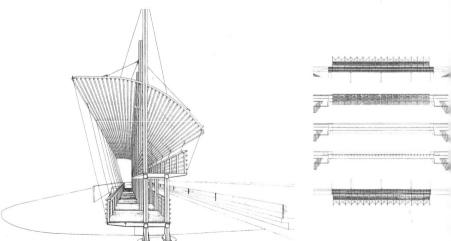

Each level of the platform defines its specific intention: one, protected and direct through the interior of the beam, provides for rapid transit, the others were designed as an urban promenade upon the beam with a scenic look-out enhanced by the beauty of the deck.

Les niveaux de passage de cette plate-forme ont plusieurs fonctions : ils offrent un rapide passage protégé à l'intérieur de la poutre, ou forment à partir de celle-ci un chemin plus paisible qui comprend une allée et un belvédère, mis en valeur grâce au toit.

Die zwei verschiedenen Höhen dieser Plattform erfüllen unterschiedliche Zwecke: der untere Weg führt geschützt und direkt zum Ziel, während die oberen zu einem Spaziergang und dem kurzen Halt am Aussichtspunkt einladen.

Its structure is based on a large metallic caisson beam. This beam sustains the upper and lower strands which support the two passage levels. These passageways, delimited by the deck, constitute a new façade overlooking Meridiana Avenue.

La structure est basée sur une grande poutre caisson, d'où partent les cordons supérieurs et inférieurs qui soutiennent les deux niveaux de passage. Ces deux niveaux, délimités par un toit, constituent une nouvelle façade sur l'Avenue.

Die Struktur der Brücke basiert auf einem großen geschlossenen Metallträger. Von ihm aus gehen überhalb und unterhalb Stahlseile aus, die zwei verschiedene Ebenen stützen und eine neue Fassade vor der Avenida bilden.

Pasarela Urbitarte

Santiago Calatrava, arq.

BILBAO, ESPAÑA. 1990

Length / Longueur / Gesamtlänge 73 m.
Span / Travée / Hauptspannweite 71 m.

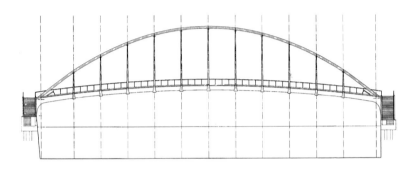

We can recognize many of the changes that the city of Bilbao has undergone over the past years by observing its architecture. Many projects by national and international firms have been encouraged: the Guggenheim Museum by Gehry, Sondika de Calatrava Airport, the Foster subway station; the construction of these works has brought a fresh and renovated image to the city. The signature of this architect is recognizable even in his pedestrian bridges as is the case of this particular footbridge. The passageway has been designed with the well-known aesthetic flare of its author, with a pattern clearly inspired by the bone structure of living beings.

Un grand nombre des changements effectués à Bilbao au cours des dernières années sont reconnaissables dans son architecture. De nombreux projets d'origine nationale et internationale ont été promus: le musée Guggenheim de Gehry, l'aéroport Sondika de Calatrava, la station de métro de Foster; leur construction a permis de renouveler et de moderniser l'image de la ville. Même dans les passages piétonniers, on reconnaît les projets d'auteur, comme c'est le cas pour cette passerelle. La conception de ce passage, à l'esthétique caractéristique de son auteur, est clairement inspirée des structures osseuses des êtres vivants.

Viele der Veränderungen, die Bilbao in den letzten Jahren erfahren hat, spiegeln sich in den architektonischen Werken der Stadt nieder. Zahlreiche Projekte unter nationaler und internationaler Leitung wurden bereits durchgeführt: das Guggenheim–Museum von Gehry, der Flughafen Sondika de Calatrava und die Metrostation Foster zum Beispiel verleihen Bilbao ein neues Gesicht. Auch an Fußgängerbrücken, wie in diesem Fall, erkennt man die neuen Tendenzen. Mit der bekannten Ästhetik des Autors verleiht er diesem Übergang eine Form, zu der ihn offensichtlich der Knochenbau eines Lebewesens inspiriert hat.

The formal design of the deck which in this case evokes the shape of a fish, reminds us of more recent projects along the same artistic line, such as the Alameda subway station or the Science Museum, both of which can be found in Valencia (Spain).

L'approche formelle de la plate-forme, semblable à un poisson, rappelle des projets plus récents conçus dans le même esprit, comme la station de métro Alameda ou le musée de la science, tous deux situés à Valence (Espagne).

Die formelle Planung der Plattform, in diesem Fall der Form eines Fisches nachempfunden, erinnert uns an andere aktuelle Designs wie die Metrostation Alameda oder das Wissenschaftsmuseum, beide erbaut in Valencia (Spanien).

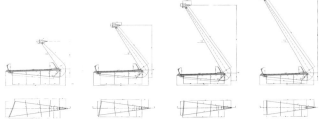

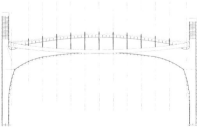

Ponte sullo Stretto di Messina

Stretto di Messina S.p.A.

SICILIA (CALABRIA), ITALIA. 1990

Length / Longueur / Gesamtlänge 3660 m.
Span / Travée / Hauptspannweite 3300 m.

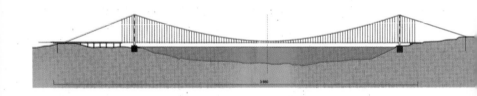

T he importance of the construction of a link between the island of Sicily and the continent passing through the region of Calabria has been studied since 1969; indeed, the international competition for ideas promoted by the transit authority A.N.A.S. dates from this year. At the moment the route between these two areas is covered by a variety of means; nonetheless, with the construction of this bridge over the Strait of Messina, still in the designing stage, it will be possible to cross over the route in only 3 minutes. The immediate consequence expected includes important changes in the area on all levels: changes in tourism, commerce, infrastructures and urban reorganization.

C' est en 1969 que l'on commence à étudier l'importance de la construction d'une liaison entre la Sicile et le continent par la région de Calabre. Cette même année, en effet, a lieu le concours international des idées, promu par l'autorité routière A.N.A.S. Le parcours d'un point à l'autre s'effectue aujourd'hui de diverses manières, mais avec la construction d'un pont sur le détroit de Messine, actuellement en projet, 3 minutes suffiront à traverser le pont. On espère, comme conséquence immédiate, d'importants changements dans la zone à tous les niveaux : touristiques, commerciaux, par rapport aux infrastructures et à la réorganisation urbaine.

S chon vor langer Zeit h man die Wichtigkeit ein Verbindung zwischen d Insel Sizilien und dem Festland d Region Kalabrien erkannt; daru fand 1969 ein international Wettbewerb um ihren Bau statt, d von der hiesigen Verkehrsverw tung A.N.A.S. organisiert wurde. Moment ist es noch recht aufwe dig, die Distanz zwischen den beid Punkten zu überwinden. Wenn all dings die sich noch im Bau befind che Brücke über die Meerenge v Messina fertiggestellt ist, wird nur noch 3 Minuten dauern d Strecke zurückzulegen. Als sofortie Konsequenz werden einige wich ge Veränderungen in der Gegend wartet, die sich zum Beispiel a touristischer, kommerzieller, infra truktureller und besiedlungstech scher Ebene bemerkbar mach werden.

This design, which will cross the strait in a single span, proposes a spacious metallic deck 60,4 m. wide with room for two railway lines in the middle and two lateral passageways with three lanes each as well as additional emergency channels.

Ce pont, qui traverse d'un seul tronçon tout le détroit, dispose d'une grande plate-forme métallique de 60,4 m de large avec deux voies ferrées au centre, deux passages latéraux formés de trois voies chacun, et des canaux d'urgence.

Dieses Projekt, das seine Gesamtlänge an einem Stück zurücklegt, besitzt eine 60,4 m breite metallische Plattform mit zwei Zugschienen im Zentrum, zwei seitlichen Fahrbahnen mit jeweils drei Spuren und zusätzliche Kanäle für Notfälle.

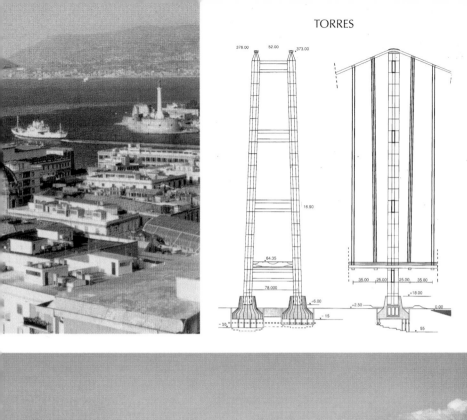

TORRES

Puente industrial «Camy-Nestle»

Enric Miralles, arq.
Se Duch, E. Prats, F. Pla, M. Martorell, J. Artigues, arq.; BOMA, est.

VILADECANS (BARCELONA), ESPAÑA. 1990-1994

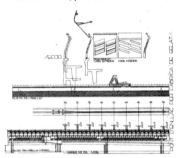

The basic function of this connecting piece, located between two buildings in an industrial plant, has been improved by its capacity as transportation element: two rails installed on this bridge accelerate considerably the transport of industrial material and electrical supply for internal use. This can be seen both in the materials used as well as in the cross-section of the bridge, where we can easily identify the three levels of passage: a concrete pedestrian lane, the industrial rails alongside it covered with metallic sheets and on the outside, overhead, a triangular structure which is used to transport electrical materials.

La fonction basique de cet élément de communication entre deux bâtiments d'une fabrique est renforcée par sa compétence en tant qu'élément transporteur : ses deux rails facilitent considérablement le transfert de matériel industriel et de fournitures électriques d'usage interne. Ceci est démontré à la fois par les matériaux utilisés et par la section même du projet, où l'on peut identifier les trois niveaux de connexion : un passage piéton en béton côtoyé par des rails industriels recouverts d'une plaque métallique, et du côté extérieur, en haut, la structure triangulaire pour le transport de matériel électrique.

Die Hauptfunktion dieses Verbindungselements zwischen zwei Gebäuden einer Fabrik besteht in der Beschleunigung des Materialaustauschs: die zwei Schienen der Brücke vereinfachen den Transport von Materialien und Rohstoffen bedeutend. Die Brücke bietet drei verschiedene Ebenen des Übergangs, diedrei verschiedene Funktionen erfüllen: eine aus Beton für Fußgänger, neben ihr findendie Industrieschienen, deren Ebene in Metall gehüllt ist, ihren Platz und im oberen Teil der dreieckigen Struktur werden Elektromaterialien transportiert.

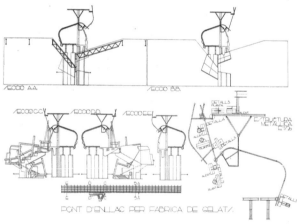

PONT D'ENLLAC PER FABRICA DE GELATS.

We can easily identify the different levels of passage from the outside: metallic sheets define the railway passage through the interior, concrete delimits the pedestrian path and the external metallic structure crowns the bridge.

Les niveaux de connexion peuvent être observés de l'extérieur : la plaque métallique définit intérieurement le passage des rails, le béton délimite le passage piétons, et la structure métallique extérieure couronne le pont.

Schon von außen sind die verschiedenen Ebenen leicht auszumachen: die Metallhülle markiert eindeutig den Weg der Schienen und der Beton den Fußweg. Die Brücke wird außerdem von einer weiteren Metallstruktur "gekrönt".

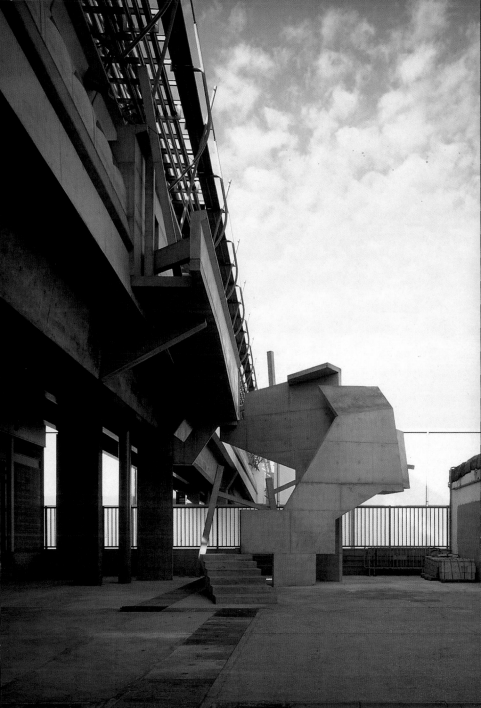

The rails are supported by a metallic structure, the concrete pedestrian deck is perforated along one side to allow the passage of light into the bridge while the triangular structure on the outside transports electrical material.

Les rails sont soutenus par une structure métallique; la plate-forme piétonne en béton s'ouvre sur le côté pour laisser passer la lumière sur toute la longueur du pont, et la structure triangulaire extérieure sert à transporter le matériel électrique.

Die Schienen finden auf einem Metallgerüst ihren Halt, die Seiten der Fußgängerplattform sind mit Öffnungen versehen, um deren Beleuchtung zu gewährleisten und die dreieckige Struktur oberhalb wird zum Transport der Elektromaterialien genutzt.

Halcrow-SEE
Laing / GTM; Freyssinet

ESTUARIO DE SEVERN (WALES), UNITED KINGDOM. 1990-1996

Length / Longueur / Gesamtlänge 948 m.
Span / Travée / Hauptspannweite 456 m.

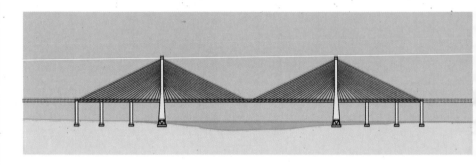

Frequently the conditions which are present at the moment of designing a bridge can transform the project into a tremendous exploit of civil engineering. This is the case of the Severn Crossing, where strong winds and vicious currents turned the project into a most delicate structural study. Due to the need to keep the actual work within the estuary to a minimum, the great majority of the components were standard pieces; thus the transport of long and heavy materials was fundamental to the construction. The great deck is made up of prefabricated factory elements which were later assembled in construction. This fact is what makes this project a particularly important achievement in the field of engineering.

Il arrive souvent que les conditions qui entourent la conception d'un pont font que ce projet se transforme en un grand effort d'ingénierie civile. C'est le cas du pont sur le Severn, où la force des vents et des courants a imposé une étude structurale minutieuse. Des pièces basiques ont été utilisées afin de minimiser les travaux sur l'estuaire. Le transport de matériaux larges et lourds a été d'une importance capitale à la construction. La grande plate-forme est constituée d'éléments préfabriqués en atelier et ensuite assemblés ; ce projet est une réussite par rapport aux ingénieries utilisées.

In Fällen, in denen die Brückenbauer besonders schwierige Bedingungen gegenüberstehen, sind oft ingenieurtechnische Meisterwerke gefragt. Beim Beispiel der Brücke über den Severn erschwerten die starken Winde und Böen die Strukturstudien des Projekts. Durch die Notwendigkeit der Geringhaltung der Arbeiten in der Trichtermündung wurden hauptsächlich Standardteile benutzt, was den Transport von schweren und langen Materialien bei den Bauarbeiten unabdingbar machte. Die große Plattform besteht aus vorgefertigten Elementen, die im Nachhinein zusammengefügt wurden, was dieses Projekt zu einem großen Erfolg für die beteiligten Ingenieure macht.

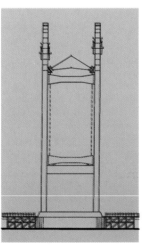

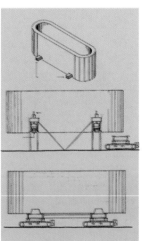

This passageway with a total length of 5168 m. is composed of two viaducts and a cable-stayed bridge. Almost all of the deck components are prefabricated pieces which were subsequently transported to the construction site; the piles constitute one of the few elements constructed in situ.

Ce passage, d'une longueur totale de 5168 m, comprend deux viaducs et un pont à haubans. La plupart des pièces qui constituent la plate-forme sont préfabriquées pour être ensuite mises en œuvre ; ses pilots comptent parmi le peu d'éléments fabriqués in situ.

Diese Brücke misst eine Gesamtlänge von 5168 m und besteht aus 2 Viadukten und einer Schrägseilbrücke. Fast alle Teile der Plattform wurden vorgefertigt und dann vor Ort montiert; die Piloten sind eins der wenigen Produkte, die direkt am Standort gefertigt wurden.

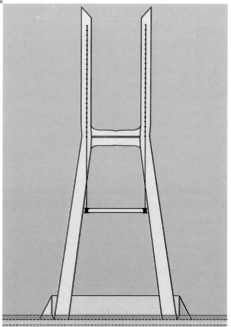

Great Belt East Bridge

Dissing+Weitling, arq.
CBR (Cowi+Ramboll), ing.

Great Belt Link; Coinfra SpA; Parsons; Skanska;
Hochtief; Hojgaard & Schultz; Monberg & Thorsen A/S

HALSSKOV-SPROGOE, DENMARK. 1990-1998.

Length / Longueur / Gesamtlänge 6790 m.
Span / Travée / Hauptspannweite 1642 m.

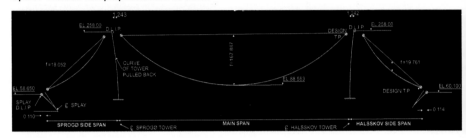

When the construction of a bridge involves overcoming natural barriers, not only are we merely joining two points but also, at times, we are responsible for the actual expansion of a country. With the construction of the Great Belt Bridge, the country of Denmark, composed of numerous islands, has succeeded in optimizing its commercial relationships with the world. This light and elegant suspension bridge, one of the largest built in recent years, has condensed to a mere 10 minutes a journey between two shores which formerly required over an hour. In addition it permits the route from southern Europe to be followed without interruption.

Quand construire un pont permet de surmonter les frontières naturelles, cela signifie non seulement la connexion entre deux points, mais parfois aussi l'expansion d'un pays entier. Le Danemark, formé de nombreuses îles, a réussi, avec la construction du Great Belt Bridge, à optimiser ses relations commerciales avec le reste du monde. Ce pont suspendu léger et élégant, un des plus grands récemment construit, permet de rejoindre en seulement 10 minutes deux rives qu'une heure de trajet séparait auparavant. En outre, grâce à cette construction, le trajet à partir du sud de l'Europe peut désormais s'effectuer de manière ininterrompue.

Wenn man mit einer Brücke eine natürliche Grenze überwindet, werden nicht immer nur lediglich zwei Punkte miteinander verbunden, sondern in manchen Fällen bringt eine Brücke auch die Expansion eines Landes mit sich. Dänemark, ein Land das aus zahlreichen Inseln besteht, hat durch den Bau der Great Belt Bridge seine Wirtschaftsbeziehungen mit der Welt optimieren können. Diese leichte und elegante Hängebrücke, eine der größten die in den letzten Jahren errichtet wurden, verbindet zwei Ufer über einen 10 Minuten langen Weg miteinander, die vorher 1 Stunde trennten. Außerdem ermöglicht sie die kontinuierliche Durchfahrt von Südeuropa aus.

This project was built following the structural concept of the suspension bridge, possibly one of the airiest bridges in appearance. This is the reason for the elegance and grace of this project, one of the longest built in recent years.

Ce projet a été construit suivant le concept structurel du pont suspendu, probablement l'un des plus légers d'un point de vue visuel. Elégant et svelte, il est l'un des ponts plus longs construit ces dernières années.

Dieses Projekt wurde unter dem strukturellen Konzept einer Hängebrücke durchgeführt, möglicherweise ist es die visuell am leichtesten erscheinende überhaupt. Darauf basiert auch die Eleganz dieser Brücke, die einer der längsten Bauten der letzten Jahren ist.

Pasarela peatonal en Petrer

Carme Pinós, arq.
J.A. Andreu, M. Lluch, C. Pascual, J. Schneider, arq.; M. Llorens, est.

PETRER (ALICANTE), ESPAÑA. 1991-1999

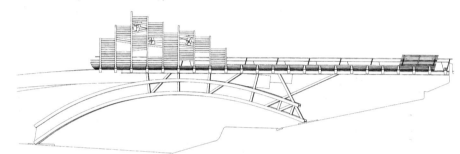

The construction of this footbridge brought with it implications beyond that of merely providing a passageway. The area chosen, a rather chaotic region located between the countryside and a town, acquired a new reference point thanks to the project. In addition to providing a passage, this footbridge became a meeting point between the two localities. The entire proposal began with a number of diverse elements and materials which were gradually moulded into what would eventually become the different components of the bridge: the lighting blends in with the pergola, the pavement rises up in curvaceous forms which transform themselves into benches while incisions make room for seats.

En plus de servir de connexion, cette passerelle a d'autres implications par rapport à l'endroit où elle a été construite. Elle a su donner une nouvelle dimension à ce lieu chaotique, situé entre une zone rurale et un village. En plus de permettre le passage, cette passerelle a la fonction d'organe de liaison entre les deux points. Le projet entier est basé sur des éléments et des matériaux modelables qui se convertissent successivement en différentes pièces : l'éclairage se fond avec la pergola, le plancher se soulève pour prendre des formes incurvées et se métamorphoser en bancs, et les incisions permettent d'inclure les sièges.

Außer der Verknüpfung zweier Punkte, bringt diese Brücke noch weitere Vorteile für die Gegend, in der sie gebaut wurde, mit sich. Der eher chaotische Standort zwischen einem Dorf und einem ländlichen Gebiet erhält einen neuen Referenten durch dieses Projekt. Es bietet außer einer bloßen Überbrückung zusätzlich einen Artikulationsbereich zwischen den zwei bisher getrennten Seiten. Das gesamte Modell entsteht aus Elementen und Materialien, die sich so formen, dass sie nach und nach in die einzelnen Teile übergehen: die Beleuchtung wird Teil der hölzernen Pergola, und aus der kurvigen Plattform gehen Bänke und Sitzgelegenheiten hervor.

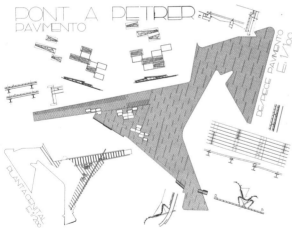

PONT A PETRER
PAVIMENTO

DESPIECE PAVIMENTO E 1/100

PLANTA GENERAL E 1/20

The approach to the project, handling it as if it were but one single piece, leads to an evocative use of materials. Thus the Iroko wood and the metallic pieces meld together and mould themselves into each of the distinctive components of the bridge.

L'élaboration de ce projet, comme s'il s'agissait d'un seul élément, favorise l'utilisation suggestive du matériel: le bois d'iroko et les pièces métalliques se fondent et se moulent pour former chacun des composants du pont.

Dieses Projekt wurde so gestaltet, dass die verwendeten Baumaterialien perfekt harmonisieren und so ineinander übergehen, dass man den Eindruck bekommt, die Brücke wäre aus einem Stück entstanden. Sie besteht allerdings aus Irokoholz und Metall.

Reinforced concrete walls support the weight of the footbridge which is formed of three metallic arches sustaining the deck, with Iroko wood pavement. The pergola, also of metal and wood, rises up above the deck.

Des murs en béton armé supportent la structure de la passerelle, formée de trois arcs métalliques qui soutiennent la plate-forme, en revêtement de bois d'iroko. Au-dessus s'élève la pergola, également faite de métal et de bois.

Die Struktur der Brücke, die aus drei Metallbögen und einer Plattform mit einem Gehweg aus Irokoholz besteht, wird von Spannbetonmauern gestützt. Die Pergola, die einen Teil der Brücke überdacht, besteht ebenfalls aus Metall und Holz.

Brücke Suderelbe

DSD Dilinger Stahlbau GmbH

HAMBURG, DEUTSCHLAND. 1992

Length / Longueur / Gesamtlänge 340,4 m.
Span / Travée / Hauptspannweite 125,61 m.

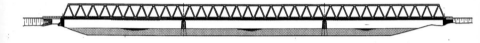

I n some cases, the ex-
isting bridges with car
and pedestrian lanes
were never designed to include railway lines. Nor do the
structure of these bridges permit an addition in order to introduce these railways and for
this reason, it is often necessary to build an entirely new
crossing. Thus, this project
originated in order to resolve
the matter of connecting the
shores of the Elbe River solely
for the passage of railway
lines, since the car and pedestrian traffic was already covered by existing bridges near-
by. The large beams proposed
for the passageway make use
of the structural advantages of
the triangle and its geometric
combinations thus creating a
stable ensemble

C ertains ponts qui
contiennent des passa-
ges pour voitures et
piétons n'envisagent pas l'in-
corporation d'une voie ferrée.
*Pour des raisons structurelles,
un élargissement à cette fin
n'est pas non plus accepté, ce
pourquoi il est souvent nécessaire de construire de nouveaux ponts. La fonction de
ce projet est d'assurer la
connexion entre les deux rives
du fleuve Elbe afin de permettre le passage de voies de train,
la circulation de voitures et de
piétons étant déjà rendue possible par les ponts avoisinants.
Les grandes poutres prévues
pour le passage utilisent les
possibilités structurelles de la
géométrie triangulaire et de ses
combinaisons, donnant ainsi
de la stabilité à l'ensemble.*

I n vielen Fällen ist es
weder möglich auf be-
reits existierenden
Auto– und Fußgängerbrücken
Schienen zu installieren noch
diese so zu erweitern, dass sie
Platz für Eisenbahnschienen
bieten. Also müssen neue
Möglichkeiten geschaffen werden. Dieses Projekt sollte eine
Verbindung zwischen den beiden Ufern der Elbe herstellen,
die die Überfahrt für Züge erlaubt, da Brücken für Autos
und Fußgänger bereits vorhan-
den waren. Die gewaltigen
Träger, die für das Projekt entworfen wurden, basieren auf
der geometrischen Form eines
Dreiecks und bilden einen
Komplex von stabilen Kon-
struktionen.

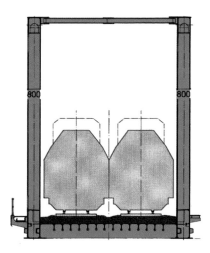

The structure of the deck was built from a metallic sheet stiffened by a series of ribs running down its entire length. Construction was carried out unilaterally starting from the north shore; the work was achieved through the use of crane barges.

La structure de la plate-forme a été construite à partir d'une planche métallique rendue rigide au moyen des nervures qui sont présentes sur toute sa longueur. Le pont a été réalisé unilatéralement à partir du côté nord, à l'aide de grues flottantes.

Die Struktur der Plattform wurde ausgehend von einer Metallplatte gebaut, die durch die Rippen, die über die gesamte Länge der Brücke angebracht worden sind, verstärkt und gestützt wird. Die Bauarbeiten wurden ausschließlich von der Nordseite her mit Schwimmkranen durchgeführt.

Natchez Trace Parkway Arches

Figg Engineering Group
Finley McNary, PCL Civil Constructors

TENNESSEE, USA. 1992-1994

Length / Longueur / Gesamtlänge 5156 m.
Span / Travée / Hauptspannweite 1909 m.

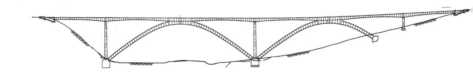

The National Parks Service of Natchez has been developing the Natchez Trace Parkway Project since the 1940's with a highway which follows the course of a route traced by the Native Americans. Hence, in 1992, this organization along with the Federal Highway Administration commissioned this project for the crossing of the valley. The bridge consists of two concrete arches, which were the first arches built in North America using prefabricated pieces for both the deck as well as the arches. The balanced proportions of the structure and its support system permitted this project to minimize its impact on the natural environment of the park.

Le Service National du Parc de Natchez a développé à partir des années 40 le projet du Natchez Trace Parkway, comprenant une autoroute qui suit le parcours marqué par les indiens d'Amérique. Ainsi en 1992, le Service National se charge de ce projet qui traverse la vallée, en collaboration avec l'Administration Fédérale des Autoroutes. Le pont est formé par deux arcs en béton, les premiers d'Amérique construits suivant le système de pièces préfabriquées, utilisées à la fois pour la plate-forme et pour les arcs. Les proportions de la structure et de son système d'appui n'ont qu'un impact minime sur l'environnement naturel du parc.

Seit den vierziger Jahren wird im National park Natchez das Natchez Trace Parkaway Projekt entwickelt, eine Schnellstraße die den Spuren der Indianischen Amerikaner folgt. In diesem Zusammenhang wurde 1992, in Zusammenarbeit mit der Federal Administration of Highways, dieses Projekt in Auftrag gegeben um ein Tal zu überbrücken. Die Brücke besteht aus zwei Betonbögen und einer Plattform, welche die ersten waren, die in Amerika nach dem Prinzip der Vorfertigung gebaut wurden. Die Proportionen der Struktur und sein Stützsystem beschränkten den Eingriff in die naturbelassene Umgebung des Nationalparks auf ein Minimum.

The arches and deck were built in their entirety with prefabricated pieces. Additional structures were used during construction which permitted building each of the arches using unidirectional cantilever.

Les arcs et la plate-forme ont été entièrement construits à l'aide de pièces préfabriquées. Des structures supplémentaires ont été utilisées pour permettre la construction en porte-à-faux unidirectionnel de chacun des arcs.

Die Bögen und die Plattform wurden einzig aus vorgefertigten Teilen zusammengefügt. Beim Bau wurden Zusatzstrukturen errichtet, die die Konstruktion der Bögen nach dem Cantilever-System in nur eine Richtung ermöglichte.

Pasarela estanque de la Cobertera

Lluis Cantallops, Miquel Simon, arq.
Lluís Mestras, ing.

Robert Brufau, arq.; X. Romaní, J. Domingo, M. Greoles, D. Closes, arq.

PASEO CALAFELL (TARRAGONA), ESPAÑA. 1992-1995

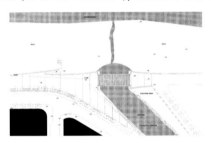

This delicate footbridge was built in order to provide continuity to the Paseo Maritimo (seaside promenade) where it crosses over Cobertera Pond. This idea also made it possible to regain a stream of water within the promenade. The choice of materials demonstrates the formal intentions of the designers: "in order to create an image of elegance and lightness the appropriate solution was a combination of a deck made of wooden boards with a metallic structure." The construction process is of special interest: the structure, built and galvanized entirely in the factory, was plated in zinc in order to prevent corrosion.

Cette passerelle élégante a été construite dans le but de donner de la continuité au Paseo Marítimo le long de l'Estanque de la Cobertera. Ce projet a aussi permis de récupérer une ligne d'eau à l'intérieur de la rue. Le choix du matériel montre les intentions formelles de ses auteurs : «pour obtenir une image de sveltesse et de légèreté, la solution idéale était la combinaison d'une plate-forme avec un plancher de bois et une structure métallique». Le procédé de construction est d'un intérêt tout particulier : entièrement construite et galvanisée en atelier, la structure a été plongée dans un bain de zinc afin d'éviter les processus corrosifs.

Dieser Übergang wurd über den Coberten Teich gebaut, um ein Verlängerung der besteher den Strandpromenade z schaffen und eine Wasserlin in den Spaziergang einzubau en. Die Auswahl der verwer deten Materialien bestärke die formalen Intentionen de Autoren der Brücke: «um de Eindruck der Leichtigkeit un Eleganz zu vermitteln, war d Kombination aus einer Hol plattform und einer Meta struktur die geeignetste L sung». Auch der Bauprozes bekam eine interessante F cette: als die Brücke vollkom men fertiggestellt und galvar siert war, wurde sie in e Zinkbad getaucht um den Ko rosionsprozess zu vermeide

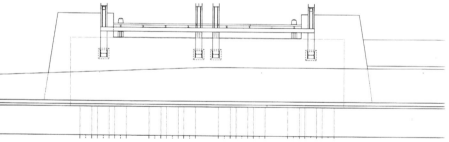

The galvanization of the structure is of great importance for its maintenance: its proximity to the sea would have made corrosion inevitable. Thus neoprene joints between the components prevented the galvanic protection from wearing off during assembly.

La galvanisation de la structure est très importante pour son entretien : très proche de la mer, la corrosion était pratiquement inévitable. Les jointures en néoprène qui séparent les pièces ont permis de conserver la protection galvanique pendant le montage.

Die Galvanisierung der Struktur ist für ihre Instandhaltung von großer Bedeutung: ihr Standort direkt am Meer würde eine starke Korrosion unvermeidlich machen. Bei der Montage wurden Neoprenschützer zwischen den Teilen angebracht, um die Beschädigung ihrer Schutzschicht zu vermeiden.

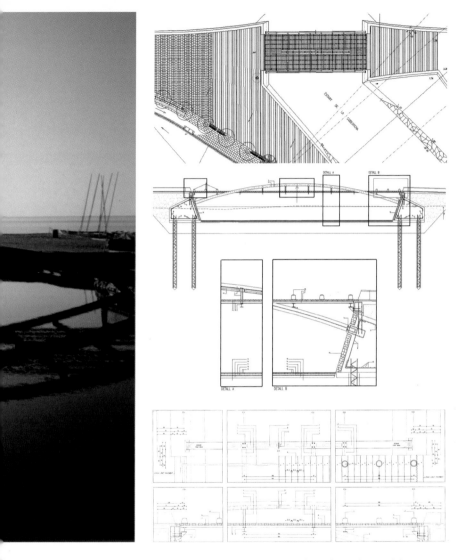

The wooden deck "suspended" from the metallic structure appears to float above the pond. In contrast we find the solid concrete and stone elements which run into the retaining walls of the pond.

La plate-forme en bois «suspendue» de la structure métallique semble flotter au-dessus du bassin. Par contraste, on observe les éléments robustes de béton et de pierre sur les murs de soutènement du bassin.

Die «hängende» Holzplattform wirkt, als würde sie auf dem Teich treiben. Als Kontrast dazu finden wir die starken Betonelemente der Schutzmauern des Gewässers.

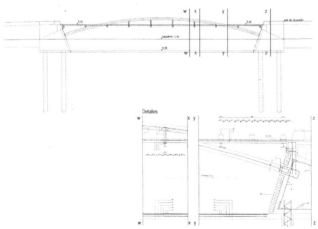

Detalles

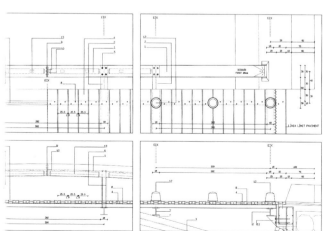

Pont de Normandie

Setra; Freyssinet; Monberg & Thorsen A/S; DSD Dillinger Stahlbau GmbH

LE HAVRE (HONEFLEUR), FRANCE. 1992-1995

Length / Longueur / Gesamtlänge 2141 m.
Span / Travée / Hauptspannweite 856 m.

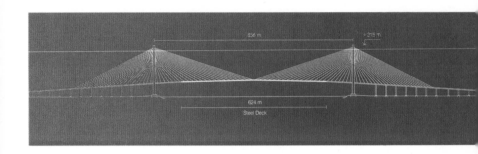

T his bridge, situated over the Seine River, is the longest cable-stayed bridge in Europe. This typology was chosen over all others as the most suitable for the conditions present in the estuary. The deck is of a combination of materials: a metallic centre span 624 m. in length is joined at each end to a concrete deck which was conceived to form a unit with the rest of the structure of the bridge. Both sides of the deck were built simultaneously on location, which exposed them to strong winds. In order to study these adverse conditions specific methods were developed to control the stability of the structure.

S itué sur la Seine, ce pont à haubans est le plus long d'Europe. Sa typologie a eu la priorité sur d'autres projets, considérée la plus adéquate par rapports aux conditions de l'estuaire. La plate-forme est mixte: une travée métallique centrale de 624 m de longueur est reliée à chaque extrémité à une travée de béton, qui forme un tout avec le reste de la structure du pont. Les côtés de la plate-forme ont été construit en même temps, et en conséquence ont été exposés à de grands vents. Des méthodes précises de contrôle de stabilité de la structure ont été développées pour étudier ces conditions.

D iese Schrägseilbrücke über dem Fluss Seine ist die längste Brücke Europas. Der gewählte Konstruktionstyp wurde anderen möglichen Bauweisen wegen der Trichtermündung des Flusses vorgezogen. Die Zusammensetzung der Plattform ist gemischt: die 624 m der metallischen Hauptspannweite vereint sich an beiden Seiten mit Betonstrukturen, die so mit dem Mittelteil verbunden wurden, dass sie eine Einheit bilden. Die beiden Seitenteile der Brücke wurden gleichzeitig gebaut und waren dabei starken Winden ausgesetzt. Um diese Einwirkungen und die Stabilität der Brücke zu kontrollieren wurden hier spezielle Methoden entwickelt.

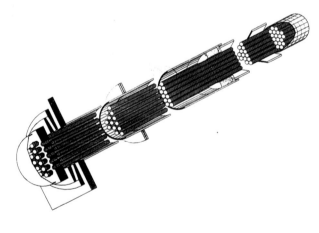

The design of an airtight casing c
the metallic span facilitates maint‹
nance. After undergoing a specif
treatment, the interior of the casin
would remain free from corrosic
while the external design, smoo‹
with simple shapes, enables th‹
maintenance process to be carrie‹
out rapidly.

Le concept d'un caisson étanch‹
dans la travée métallique facili›
l'entretien du pont. Son élabor‹
tion précise évite la corrosion c
l'intérieur du caisson, et l'extérieu
lisse et aux formes simples, fait c
l'entretien une procédure rapide.

Die Verwendung eines herm‹
tischen Metallkastens für d‹
langen Mittelteil der Plattfor‹
vereinfacht die Instandhaltun‹
Durch eine spezielle Behandlur
greift die Korrosion nie d‹
Innenteil des Kastens an, sonde
nur den glatten Außenteil, dess‹
Reinigung und Instandhaltur
unproblematisch ist.

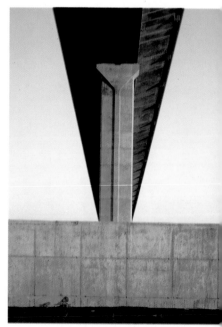

The concrete portion of the deck was designed as a structural unit along with the pylons; the metallic span was subsequently attached without the use of joints between the two materials, thus converting the surface of the roadway into one single element.

Le béton de la plate-forme a été prévu pour former une unité structurelle avec les tours. La travée métallique a été fixée plus tard, sans aucune jointure entre les deux matériaux. Ainsi, la surface de passage se transforme en un élément unique.

Der Beton der Plattform wurde als eine Einheit mit den Türmen errichtet, danach wurde der metallische Teil angebracht, wobei sich die beiden verschiedenen Oberflächen zu einem Element vereinen.

Greiner International Ltd.; Maunsell Consultants Asia Ltd; Leonhardt, Andrä und Partner.

Mott MacDonald; Flint & Neill Partnership; Sir William Halcrow and Partners Ltd.

LANTAU–HONG KONG. 1992-1997

Length / Longueur / Gesamtlänge 820 m.
Span / Travée / Hauptspannweite 430 m.

Shipping Clearance 47M

Kap Shui Mun Bridge forms a part of the highway network to Lantau Island, a route which is important for reaching the new Chek Lap Kok Airport from Hong Kong. The bridge is responsible for connecting the islands of Lantau and Ma Wan across the Kap Shui Mun Channel. Once on the island of Ma Wan it joins with the Tsing Ma Bridge. Due to the importance of the Ma Wan Viaduct, of which this bridge forms a part, its structure was designed to support the weight of the intense traffic generated in this region. Thus its deck occupies two levels: the upper level holds three lanes in each direction while the lower deck includes two protected lanes and a railway line.

Le pont Kap Shui Mun fait partie du réseau de connexion avec l'île de Lantau, route importante entre Hong Kong et le nouvel aéroport de Chek Lap Kok. Le pont passe sur le canal Kap Shui Mun et relie les îles de Lantau et de Ma Wan, pour ensuite rejoindre le pont Tsing Ma. Dû à l'importance du viaduc Ma Wan, duquel ce pont fait partie, la structure a été conçue pour supporter la circulation intense qui existe dans ce quartier. La plate-forme se projette à deux niveaux : trois voies pour chaque sens circulatoire sur la partie supérieure, et au-dessous, deux voies protégées, et une réservée aux trains.

Die Brücke Kap Shui Mun bildet Teil der Verbindung mit der Insel Lantau, eine wichtige Straße auf dem Weg von Hong Kong zum neuen Flughafen Chek Lap Kok. Über den Kanal Kap Shui Mun verbindet die Brücke die Inseln Lantau und Ma Wan, von wo aus man zur Brücke Tsing Ma gelangt. Die Kap Shui Mun ist Teil des Viadukts Ma Wan, wo der Verkehr ganz besonders dicht ist. Diesen Anforderungen entsprechend wurde natürlich die Brücke gebaut. Ihre Plattform besteht aus zwei Ebenen: der obere Teil verfügt über drei Spuren für jede Fahrtrichtung, und der untere über eine Eisenbahnschiene und zwei geschützte Fahrbahnen.

A two-level deck allows the lower level to be used in situations other than the usual ones: for example as an access for maintenance, a protected passageway during periods of strong winds or in emergency situations.

Grâce aux niveaux de la plate-forme, les deux voies inférieures peuvent être utilisées, en plus de leur fonction de base, à des fins variées : pour l'entretien, comme passages protégés en cas de vents forts ou dans des situations d'urgence.

Die Fahrspuren auf der unteren Ebene sind für eventuelle Ausnahmesituationen, wie starkem Wind, Notfällen und Instandhaltungsarbeiten, vorbehalten und bieten so eine zusätzliche Sicherheit.

The outline of the construction process shows the different stages of the work on this cable-stayed bridge, with towers 150 m. above sea-level; the tower nearest the island of Lantau received a special coating to protect it from the ships.

Le schéma de la procédure de construction montre les différentes étapes de l'élaboration de ce pont à haubans, avec des tours situées à 150 m au-dessus du niveau de la mer, dont la plus proche de Lantau est recouverte d'un revête-ment spécial pour la protéger des bateaux.

Das Schema des Bauprozesses zeigt die Etappen, in denen diese Schrägseilbrücke errichtet wurde. Die Türme messen eine Höhe von 150 m über dem Meeresspiegel wobei der, der der Insel Lantau am nächsten steht, mit einem speziellen Belag überzo-gen wurde um ihn gegen eventuelle Stöße mit Schiffen zu wappnen.

Tsing Ma Bridge

Mott MacDonald Hong Kong Limited
Flint & Neill Partnership; Sir William Halcrow and Partners Ltd.; Gleitbau Salzburg

LANTAU–HONG KONG. 1992-1997

Length / Longueur / Gesamtlänge 2160 m.
Span / Travée / Hauptspannweite 1377 m.

An important highway network exists between the island of Lantau and Hong Kong. Two bridges make up this route: the Kap Shui Mun Bridge and the Tsing Ma Bridge. The latter, the largest of the two bridges, is responsible for connecting the small island of Ma Wan with that of Tsing Yi. Moving from this island in a northerly direction, this bridge joins with the Ting Kau Bridge; subsequently, upon its arrival on the island of Ma Wan it unites with the viaduct which leads to Kap Shui Ming Bridge. In a relatively short period of time this bridge has become one of the symbols of the city of Hong Kong. For this reason a study was conducted concerning the lighting of the structure in order to further enhance its beauty as part of the landscape of the island.

Il existe entre l'île de Lantau et Hong Kong un important réseau de connexion formé de deux ponts : le Kap Shui Mun et le Tsing Ma. Ce dernier, le plus grand des deux, a pour fonction la liaison entre la petite île de Ma Wan et celle de Tsing Yi. Au nord de l'île, il rejoint le pont Ting Kau – qui va en direction de Ma Wan – et retrouve le viaduc qui mène au pont Kap Shui Mun. Ce pont est rapidement devenu l'un des symboles de la ville de Hong Kong, ce qui a donné lieu à une étude sur l'éclairage de la structure, qui a permis de mettre en valeur le paysage de l'île.

Zwischen der Insel Lantau und Hong Kong existiert ein wichtiges Verbindungsnetz, das aus zwei Brücken besteht: die Kap Shui Mun und die Tsing Ma. Die letztere ist die größere von beiden und bildet den Übergang von der kleinen Insel Ma Wan zu Tsing Yi. Im Norden dieser Insel vereint sie sich mit der Brücke Ting Kau, und bei seiner Ankunft auf der Insel Ma Wan trifft sie auf das Viadukt, das zur Brücke Kap Shui Mun führt. Innerhalb kürzester Zeit nach ihrer Fertigstellung wurde diese Brücke zu einem Symbol der Stadt Hong Kong. Um sie so noch mehr aus der Insellandschaft hervorstechen zu lassen und somit ihre Bedeutung zu betonen, hat man ein besonders starkes Beleuchtungssystem für die Brücke angebracht.

Tsing Ma Bridge is currently
the longest suspension bridge
in the world with a deck combining car lanes with railway
lines. Its two-level metallic
deck is composed entirely of
prefabricated pieces assembled during construction.

Le Tsing Ma est actuellement
le pont suspendu le plus long
du monde, avec une plate-for-
me métallique à deux niveaux,
entièrement préfabriquée et
mise en œuvre, qui permet le
passage de voitures et de
trains.

Die Tsing Ma ist heutzutage die
längste Hängebrücke der Welt,
die Autos und Zügen die Überfahrt gewährt. Ihre metallische
Plattform besteht einzig aus vorgefertigten Teilen, die vor Ort zusammengefügt wurden.

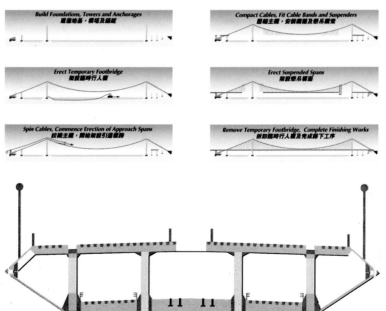

Build Foundations, Towers and Anchorages 建造地基，橋塔及錨錠	Compact Cables, Fit Cable Bands and Suspenders 壓縮主纜，安裝纜箍及懸吊纜索
Erect Temporary Footbridge 架設臨時行人橋	Erect Suspended Spans 架設懸吊橋面
Spin Cables, Commence Erection of Approach Spans 絞纜主纜，開始架設引道橋飾	Remove Temporary Footbridge, Complete Finishing Works 拆卸臨時行人橋及完成餘下工序

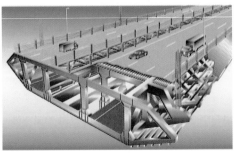

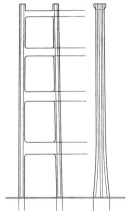

The towers of the bridge, of reinforced concrete, are 206 m. high and constructed upon each of the islands in order to facilitate the laying of foundations. The deck passes underneath each tower and is sustained by cables hanging from the towers.

La hauteur totale des tours du pont, en béton armé, équivaut à 206 m. Ces tours sont établies sur chacune des îles afin de consolider les fondations. Au milieu s'étend la plate-forme, soutenue par les câbles qui mènent aux tours.

Die Türme der Brücke, die aus Stahlbeton bestehen, sind insgesamt 206 m hoch und wurden jeweils auf den Inseln befestigt, um deren Fundamentierung zu vereinfachen. Die Plattform führt durch die Gabelung der Plattform hindurch und wird von Kabeln gehalten, die zu den Türmen reichen.

Ponte Vasco da Gama

Gatell
Lusoponte; Concepción; Novaponte; Freyssinet

LISBOA, PORTUGAL 1992, 1995-1998

Length / Longueur / Gesamtlänge 830 m.
Span / Travée / Hauptspannweite 420 m.

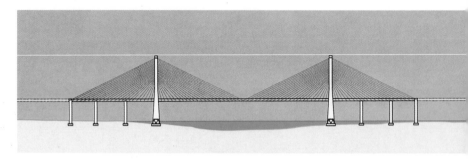

In the search for an alternative route to the 25th of April Bridge, a competition was announced for the construction of a new bridge to be inaugurated for the Lisbon World Exposition of 1998. As a result this bridge was built as part of a connection on a larger scale with other routes of different types: the north viaduct of 560 m., the Expo Viaduct of 670 m., the centre bridge of 830 m., the centre viaduct of 6500 m. and the south viaduct and access road of 4300 m. The predominant material used is concrete except for the combined deck of the cable-stayed bridge. The impact generated by this new structure makes it an important element upon the Tagus River.

Afin de trouver une alternative au pont 25 de Abril, un concours est organisé pour la construction d'un nouveau pont devant être inauguré à l'occasion de l'Exposition Universelle de Lisbonne de 1998. Ce pont est donc construit à l'intérieur d'une connexion à plus grande échelle avec d'autres voies de différents types : le viaduc nord de 560 m, le viaduc de l'Expo, de 670 m, le pont central de 830 m, le viaduc central, de 6500 m, et le viaduc sud de 4300 m. Le béton est le matériel le plus utilisé pour ce pont à haubans, à l'exception de la plate-forme mixte. L'impact causé par cette nouvelle structure en fait un élément important sur le fleuve Tage.

Auf der Suche nach einer Alternative zur Brücke 25 de Abril, wurde vor einigen Jahren der Wettbewerb um den Bau dieser Brücke durchgeführt, die rechtzeitig vor der Expo 1998 in Lissabon eingeweiht werden sollte. So wurde die Brücke im Kontext eines umfangreichen Projekts, das mehrere Trajekte verschiedener Typen einschließt, gebaut: das Nordviadukt (560 m), das Viadukt der Expo (670 m), die Zentralbrücke (670 m), das Zentralviadukt (6500 m) und das Südviadukt und seine Zufahrt mit einer Länge von 4300 m. Der Beton ist das zum größten Teil benutzte Material, mit Ausnahme der gemischten Plattform der Schrägseilbrücke. Diese neue Struktur über den Fluss Tajo stellt eine wichtige Veränderung in der Organisation des Verkehrs und auch der optischen Erscheinung der Gegend dar.

The enormous length of this new ensemble over the Tagus River makes it an important visual element in the river's landscape. The use of concrete throughout all the sections of the structure gives it its predominant colour.

La longueur de ce nouveau complexe sur le Tage fait de sa structure un important élément visuel à l'intérieur du paysage fluvial. L'emploi de béton sur toutes les parties de la structure donne la couleur prédominante du pont.

Die extreme Länge dieses neuen Brückenkomplexes über dem Tajo hat die visuelle Erscheinung der Flusslandschaft sehr verändert. Die Verwendung von Beton in allen Teilen verleiht der Struktur seine typische Farbe.

Akinada Bridge

Hiroshima Prefecture

HIROSHIMA, JAPAN. 1992-2000

Length / Longueur / Gesamtlänge 1175 m.
Span / Travée / Hauptspannweite 750 m.

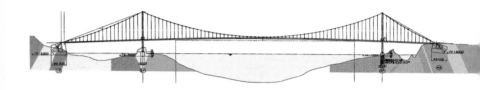

This bridge was designed with the intention of facilitating the approach to the Akinada Island group thus stimulating the commercial activity of the region as well as promoting tourism in the area. Hence this slim and delicate suspension bridge unites the different islands. Its elegance lies in the slender deck bearing only two car lanes and one pedestrian path. The proportion between the width and length of the bridge makes it appear as merely a connecting "line". Nonetheless, since this factor could have compromised the stability of the bridge, structural controls during construction were fundamental in order to complete the project successfully.

Ce pont a été conçu dans le but de faciliter l'accès à l'archipel d'Akinada et de développer ainsi l'activité commerciale en plus de promouvoir le tourisme dans cette zone. Il s'agit d'un pont suspendu léger et filiforme qui relie les différentes îles. Son élégance procède de sa fine plateforme composée de deux voies de voitures et un passage piéton seulement, qui, en proportion à sa longueur, donne à ce pont l'image d'une «ligne» de connexion. Ce facteur pourrait cependant compromettre la stabilité de cette composition, car les contrôles structurels sont restés basiques pendant la construction pour pouvoir mener à bien le projet.

Diese Brücke wurde er baut, um einen Zu gang zu den Akinada Inseln zu schaffen und somi die wirtschaftliche und touris tische Aktivität in der Gegen zu stimulieren. Eine elegante und feine Hängebrücke verein heutzutage die verschiedene Inseln. Ihre elegante Erschei nung wird vor allem von seine schmalen Plattform mit Fahrspuren für Autos und ei nem Gehweg für Fußgänge bewirkt, die die Brücke, i Proportion zu ihrer Länge, wie eine lange «Linie» erscheiner lässt. Genau aus diesem Grun war es notwendig, um da Projekt erfolgreich beende zu können, die Stabilitätskon trollen während des Baus be sonders streng zu halten.

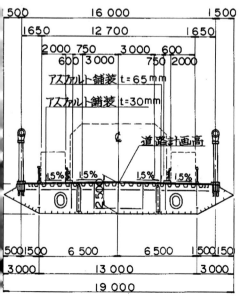

500 | 16 000 | 1 500
1650 | 12 700 | 1650
2000 750 | 3 000 600
600 3 000 | 750 2000
アスファルト舗装 t=65mm
アスファルト舗装 t=30mm
道路計画高
1.5% 1.5% 1.5% 1.5%
R=500
500 150 | 6 500 | 6 500 | 1 500 150
3 000 | 13 000 | 3 000
19 000

aThe case of the Akinada Bridge stands out due to the proportion between the width and total length of the deck which, combined with the visual lightness characteristic of this type of bridge, makes this intervention completely respectful of its surroundings.

Le pont d'Akinada est mis en exergue par le rapport qui existe entre la largeur de la plate-forme et sa longueur totale, ce qui, en plus de l'impression de légèreté, contribue au respect du milieu environnant.

Im Fall der Akinada ist die Proportion zwischen der Breite der Plattform und der Länge der Brücke ein besonders kennzeichnendes Merkmal. Die optische Leichtigkeit dieses Konstruktionstyps respektiert auch so weit wie möglich die natürliche Landschaft.

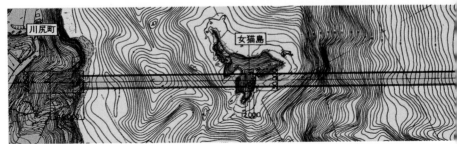

川尻町

女猫島

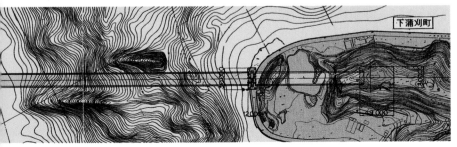

下蒲刈町

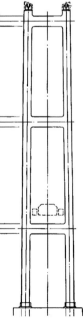

The bridge forms a part of the Akinada Highway with a total length of 2 km. It passes over the Neko-Seto Strait, a region of intense commercial activity based on the fishing industry as well as a busy shipping lane.

Ce pont, d'une longueur totale de 2 km, fait partie de la route Akinada. Il passe au-dessus du détroit de Neko-Seto, zone d'activité commerciale intense basée sur la pêche, et ligne maritime très fréquentée.

Die Brücke mit einer Gesamtlänge von 2 km ist Teil der Schnellstraße Akinada. Sie führt über die Meerenge von Neko-Seto, eine Gegend in der die Fischerei von großer Bedeutung ist und die auch einen vielbefahrener Seeweg darstellt.

Pont Antrenas

P. Dezeuze, arq.; SETRA: M. Virlogeux, Bouchon, J. Resplendino, Berthellemy.
État, A. Bourjot

ST.LAURENT DE MURET-ANTRENAS, FRANCE. 1993

Length / Longueur / Gesamtlänge 86 m.

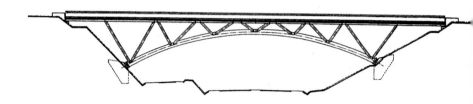

On Highway A75 near Antrenas we find this bridge which connects St. Laurent de Muret with Antrenas. The structure consists of a metallic arch 56 m. wide, circular in shape, supporting a group of tubular pipes – a product of triangulation – which bear the weight of the concrete deck. The structural simplicity creates the formal image of the bridge which bases itself upon the arch as the principal element. This arch is visible long before arriving at the bridge. The use of red in the metallic pieces and the concrete in its original shade confer a delicate colouring to the project.

Sur la voie rapide A 75, à hauteur d'Antrenas, se trouve ce pont, chargé de relier Saint Laurent de Muret et Antrenas. Sa structure est composée d'un arc de 56 m de large à section circulaire, qui regroupe des tubulaires – produit de la triangulation – sur lesquels repose la plate-forme de béton. La simplicité structurelle engendre l'image formelle de ce pont, où l'arc constitue l'élément principal, que l'on peut apercevoir de loin. L'emploi du rouge pour les éléments métalliques, et du béton dans sa couleur originale, donne une teinte délicate à cette structure.

Auf der Autobahn A 7? in der Höhe von Ar trenas, finden wir die se Brücke, die eine Verbindun zwischen St. Laurent de Mure und Antrenas herstellt. Di Struktur besteht aus einem 5 m breiten metallischen Boge mit kreisförmigen Querschnit der eine Gruppe von Röhre –Produkte der Triangulation aufnimmt, die wiederum di Brückenplattform stützt, di aus Beton besteht. Die struktu relle Einfachheit ist charakteris tisch für diese Brücke und wir vor allem durch den Bogen al ihr Hauptelement vermittel die durch ihre rote Färbun schon von Weitem ins Aug fällt.

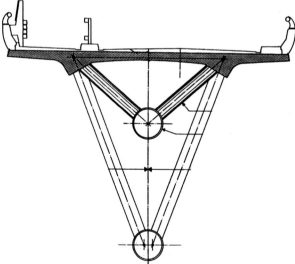

The cross-section of the deck shows how the structure works: tubular pipes of a design based on triangulation rise up out of the circular-shaped metallic arch. These pipes transmit the weight borne by the concrete deck.

La section de la plate-forme montre le fonctionnement de la structure: les tubulaires conçus sur la base de la triangulation partent de l'arc métallique à section circulaire, et supportent le poids de la plate forme de béton.

Die Funktionsweise dieser Brücke ist die folgende: an dem Metallbogen mit kreisförmigem Querschnitt sind die Röhren, die nach dem Prinzip der Triangulation entworfen wurden, befestigt, die die Plattform und die von ihr empfangenen Ladungen stützt.

Humboldthafen Brücke

Architeckten von Gerkan, Marg und Partner
Schlaich Bergermann und Partner;
DSD Dillinger Stahlbau GmbH

BERLIN, DEUTSCHLAND 1993

Length / Longueur / Gesamtlänge 245 m.

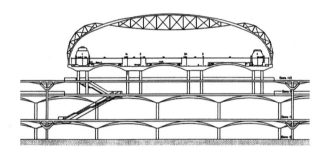

In 1993 the architect Meinhard von Gerkan and his team won first prize in the competition for the design of Lehrter Station, an emblematic area in the city of Berlin, which in turn is the intersection for railway lines arriving from different parts of the country. The project for the station, whose image is characterized by a delicate deck of steel and glass, also includes Humboldthafen Bridge, designed in accordance with the formal intentions of the station as a whole: a group of metallic arches, appearing for the first time on a railway bridge and resting upon pre-stressed concrete foundations, sustain the deck.

En 1993, l'architecte Meinhard von Gerkan et son équipe remportent le premier prix d'un concours pour la conception de la gare de Lehrter, lieu emblématique de la ville de Berlin, point d'intersection des lignes ferroviaires de tout le pays. Le projet pour cette gare, au toit raffiné mêlant verre et acier, inclut également le pont Humboldthafen, conçu suivant les intentions formelles de l'ensemble : un groupe d'arcs métalliques, utilisés pour la première fois pour un pont ferroviaire, qui reposent sur des fondations en béton précontraint soutenant la plate-forme.

Im Jahr 1993 gewannen der Architekt Meinhard von Gerkan und sein Team den ersten Preis im Wettbewerb um den Entwurf des Bahnhofs Lehrter, ein markanter Ort innerhalb der Stadt Berlin, der eine wichtige Kreuzung mehrerer Eisenbahnlinien des Landes darstellt. Teil des Projekts des Bahnhofs, dessen Charakter hauptsächlich durch eine feine Kuppel aus Glas und Stahl geprägt wird, ist auch die Humboldthafen Brücke, die im Einklang mit dem architektonischen Charakter des Komplexes steht: eine Gruppe von Metallbögen, die dieser Art erstmals für eine Eisenbahn-brücke verwendet wurden, in einem Fundament aus Stahlbeton halten die Brückenplattform

365

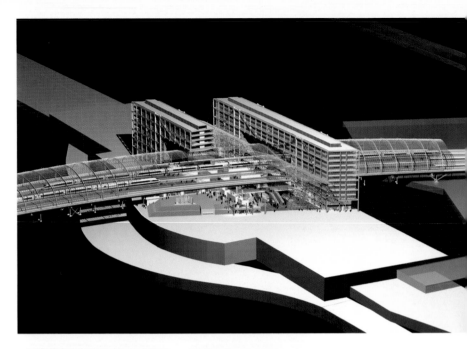

The structure of Lehrter Station fulfils various functions: on the one hand it serves as connection between different railway lines and, on the other hand, it is the urban connection between the city and other districts.

Le complexe de la gare de Lehrter a plusieurs fonctions: il sert d'une part de connexion entre les différentes lignes ferroviaires, et à échelle urbaine, il assure la liaison entre la ville et ses districts.

Der Komplex des Bahnhofs Lehrter erfüllt zwei wichtige Zwecke: einerseits dient er als Verknüpfungspunkt mehrerer Eisenbahnlinien und andererseits als Verbindung zwischen der Stadt und dem Rest des Landes.

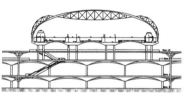

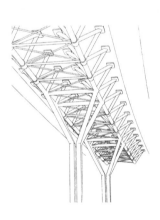

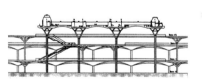

Footbridge in Museumpark

Office for Metropolitan Architecture
Y. Brunier; P. Blaisse; R. Koolhaas & T. Adam; M. Lammers; G. Mescherowsky
ROTTERDAM, HOLLAND. 1994

This footbridge located in Museumpark forms a part of a linear path divided into 5 sections: at both ends of the pathway, a group of buildings (the Architecture Institute and the Kunsthaal) and in between the buildings, 3 open air spaces which constitute the park. Nonetheless the route between these 3 sections is based upon the sensation of continuity rather than on a spatial division. For this reason, although the footbridge forms a part of the main pathway the attention is directed towards the beauty of the area. Consequently we find ourselves before an almost imperceptible structure and a delicate handling of the ground which emphasizes the lighting contrasts in the area.

Cette passerelle est située à l'intérieur du Museumpark. Elle fait partie d'un parcours linéaire divisé en cinq sections : à chaque extrémité, les bâtiments (l'Institut d'Architecture et le Kunsthaal) et au milieu, trois espaces en plein air qui forment le parc. Néanmoins, le passage entre ces trois sections est basé sur la continuité et non sur la différence spatiale. Pour cette raison, bien que la passerelle constitue le parcours principal, c'est sur la beauté du site que l'attention se porte. Nous nous trouvons face à une structure presque imperceptible et une élaboration soignée du sol qui met en évidence les contrastes lumineux du parc.

Diese Fußgängerbrücke im Museumpark ist Teil einer Tour durch den Park, die in 5 Abschnitte gegliedert werden kann: an beiden Enden befinden sich die Gebäude (Institut für Architektur und die Kunsthaal) und dazwischen verteilen sich 3 Flächen unter freiem Himmel, die den Park bilden und die 5 Abschnitte miteinander verbinden. Obwohl die Fußgängerbrücke Teil des Hauptweges des Parks ist, richtet sich das Augenmerk des Besuchers eher auf die Schönheit des Ortes im Allgemeinen. Darum wurde hier eine wenig aufsehenerregende Struktur gewählt, deren Plattform die vorhandenen Lichtkontraste innerhalb des Parks noch verstärkt.

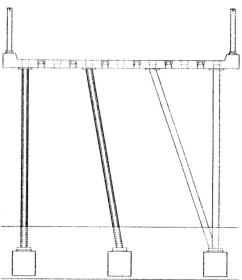

The stroll from one building to another takes us through the park which includes this footbridge. The handling of all the elements permits this structure to introduce itself delicately into the park in order to enhance the beauty of the area.

Le trajet d'un bâtiment à un autre s'effectue à travers le parc où passe cette passerelle. L'élaboration de chacun de ses éléments permet à la structure de s'introduire discrètement dans le parc et de faire ressortir la beauté de ce lieu.

Der Weg von einem Gebäude zum anderen führt durch den Park, in dem wir diese Brücke finden. Sie fügt sich dezent in die Landschaft des Parks ein, um dessen Schönheit hervorzuheben.

Wandre Bridge

René Greisch, ing.

WANDRE (HERSTAL), BELGIQUE. 1994

Length / Longueur / Gesamtlänge 408 m.
Span towards Albert Channel / Travée vers le Canal Albert / Abschnitt zum Albert-Kanal 168 m.
Span towards Mosal River / Travée vers la Rivière Mosal / Abschnitt zur Mosel 168 m.

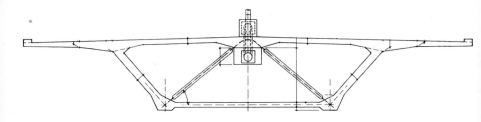

Wandre Bridge forms a part of a complex project of highway networks crossing Albert Canal and the Mosa River, with the intention of joining the industrial area of Liege with the port of Antwerp. This bridge arose as a replacement for two bridges which were demolished: the Esperanto Bridge and the old Wandre Bridge. The location of the site and the demands of the project created certain restrictions, such as the necessity of establishing a clearance over the water for navigation, and the need to avoid placing supports within the canal while limiting those within the river to a single support. Thus the result is a structure which boasts a single pylon which, along with the supporting cables running from it, supports all the weight of the decks of this bridge.

Le Wandre Bridge fait partie d'un projet complexe de réseau routier passant par le canal Albert et par la Meuse, avec pour objectif la connexion entre la zone industrielle de Liège et le port d'Anvers. Ce pont a été crée pour succéder aux deux ponts qui avaient été démolis : l'Esperanto et l'ancien Wandre. La situation géographique et les exigences du projet ont impliqué des restrictions, comme la nécessité d'une hauteur libre au-dessus de l'eau ou encore l'interdiction d'utiliser des appuis sur le canal, ou seulement un sur la rivière. Le résultat est une structure avec une tour unique, dont les tenseurs qui la rejoignent supportent les plates-formes de ce pont.

Die Wandre Bridge ist Teil eines komplexen Projekts der Straßenbaukunst über den Albert Canal und die Mosel mit dem Zweck, das Industriegebiet von Liege mit dem Hafen von Antwerpen zu verbinden. Diese Brücke wurde als Ersatz für zwei geschaffen, die abgerissen wurden: die Esperanto und die alte Wandre. Die örtlichen Gegebenheiten und die speziellen Wünsche des Auftraggebers erschwerten das Projekt. Es durfte zum Beispiel eine bestimmte freie Höhe über dem Wasser nicht unterschritten werden; außerdem sollte kein Brückenpfeiler im Kanal und höchstens einer im Fluss gebaut werden. Das Ergebnis der Planungen wurde also ein Projekt mit nur einem Turm der, zusammen mit den Spannern, die an ihm befestigt sind, die Plattform halten.

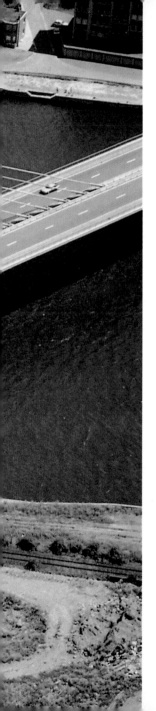

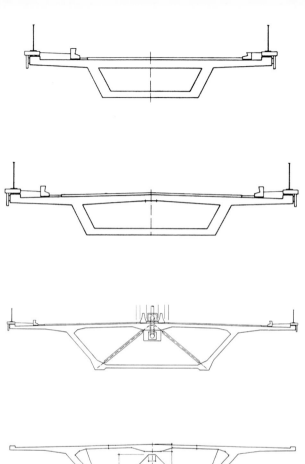

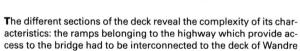

The different sections of the deck reveal the complexity of its characteristics: the ramps belonging to the highway which provide access to the bridge had to be interconnected to the deck of Wandre Bridge as one single unit.

Les différentes sections de la plate-forme témoignent de la complexité de ses caractéristiques – les rampes qui appartiennent à la route et qui permettent l'accès au pont devaient former un tout avec le Wandre Bridge.

Die Bauweise der verschiedenen Sektionen der Plattform ist besonders komplex; die Rampen, die zur Straße gehören und die Zufahrt zur Brücke gewähren, bilden eine Einheit mit der Fahrbahn, die durch die Wandre Bridge geschaffen wurde.

The structure of the bridge consisting of one single pylon helps to provide the necessary width to the lighting as seen from both the canal as well as the river, which permits the deck to stand with a minimum of supports.

La structure du pont, avec sa tour unique, contribue à obtenir une variété de lumières nécessaires à la fois sur le canal et sur la rivière, avec un minimum d'appuis au niveau de la plate-forme.

Der mächtige, einzige Turm der Brücke macht es möglich, die Plattform mit einem Minimum an Stützen zu halten und hilft auch bei der Ausstattung der Struktur mit der notwendigen Beleuchtung.

Ting Kau Bridge

Ting Kau Contractors; Schlaich Bergermann und Partner; Binnie Consultants Ltd.
Flint & Neill Partnership; Messrs.Sandberg;
Hyder Consulting Ltd.; Freyssinet

TSING YI, HONG KONG. 1994-1998

Length / Longueur / Gesamtlänge 1177 m.
Span / Travée / Hauptspannweite 477 m.

J ust as the construction of bridges can contribute to the economic development of a region, the reverse can also be true: as a result of economic development it becomes possible to build grand structures which optimize interchange. In Asia, where many countries include numerous islands this process of interchange is based on the fundamental necessity for connection. Ting Kau Bridge, one of the few cable-stayed bridges with three pylons, joins Tai Lam Tunnel with the island of Tsing Yi where it becomes a part of the connecting network with the island of Lantau, this latter composed of Kap Shui Ming and Tsing Ma Bridges.

D e même manière que la construction de ponts peut contribuer au développement économique d'une région, le processus inverse peut aussi avoir lieu : le développement économique peut rendre possible la construction de grandes structures qui optimisent cet échange. En Asie, où de nombreux pays sont formés d'îles, les connexions constituent des besoins de base. Le pont Ting Kau, l'un des seuls ponts à haubans composé de trois tours, a pour fonction de relier le tunnel Tai Lam à l'île de Tsing Yi, où il rejoint le réseau de connexion avec l'île de Lantau, constituée des ponts Kap Shui Mun et Tsing Ma.

S o wie der Bau eine Brücke zur wirtschaft lichen Entwicklung ei ner Region beitragen kann, is auch der umgekehrte Effek oft spürbar: die wirtschaftliche Weiterentwicklung ermöglich den Bau neuer, größere Brücken, um den Austausch zu optimieren. In Asien, wo viele Länder aus Inseln bestehen basieren diese Prozesse of auf der grundlegender Notwendigkeit der Verbindung Die Ting Kau, eine der weniger Schrägseilseilbrücken mit dre Türmen, verbindet den Tunne Tai Lam mit der Insel Tsing Yi um dort Anschluss an die Kar Shui Mun und die Tsing Ma zu finden, der Brückenkomplex der den Zugang zur Inse Lantau ermöglicht.

The passage deck is divided into two sections which interconnect and are hung from each side of the pylons by a total of 384 guylines. This system improves the functioning of the structure in the presence of strong winds.

La plate-forme de passage se divise en deux sections qui se rejoignent et s'interrompent de chaque côté des tours avec 384 tenseurs au total. Ce système permet un meilleur fonctionnement de la structure face aux vents.

Die Brückenplattform ist durch die Position der Türme in zwei Hälften geteilt, die untereinander verbunden sind und mit 384 Spannern befestigt wurden. Dieses System garantiert eine bessere Funktionstüchtigkeit der Struktur auch bei starken Winden.

Millenium Bridge

Foster and Partners, Sir Anthony Caro, Ove Arup & Partners

K. Shutleworth, A. Bow, C. Ramsden, J. Salero, arq.

LONDON, UNITED KINGDOM. 1994-2000

Length / Longueur / Gesamtlänge 320 m.
Span / Travée / Hauptspannweite 144 m.

From the beginning the sculptor Anthony Caro and the engineer Ove Arup were involved in this project which won an international competition. For this reason the resulting design is that of a delicate connecting element which reflects the dialectic between art, architecture and engineering. This slender passageway has become the symbol of the regeneration of the southern district with Tate Modern and the Globe Theatre on one shore, and the revitalization of the northern area with St. Paul's Cathedral on the other. If the bridge was conceived from the beginning as an urban space from which to admire the city, the construction of Tate Modern will transform it into one of the most vital areas over the Thames River.

A ce projet, qui remporte le premier prix lors d'un concours international, ont participé dès le début le sculpteur Anthony Caro et l'ingénieur Ove Arup. Le résultat est un élément de connexion élégant qui reflète la dialectique entre l'art, l'architecture et l'ingénierie. Ce pont élancé symbolise le renouveau de la zone sud, avec la Tate Modern et le Globe Theatre d'un côté, et de l'autre, la redynamisation du nord, avec la cathédrale St. Paul. D'abord conçu comme un espace urbain à partir duquel on peut admirer la ville, il deviendra avec la construction de la Tate Modern l'un des endroits les plus importants sur la Tamise.

An diesem Projekt, das bei einem internationalen Wettbewerb vergeben wurde, nahmen der Bildhauer Anthony Caro und die Ingenieure von Ove Arup teil. Diese Zusammenarbeit wird deutlich am Resultat sichtbar, das die Dialektik zwischen Kunst, Architektur und Ingenieurwesen widerspiegelt Dieser elegante Übergang ist zum Symbol für die Regenerierung des Südens, mit der Tate Modern und dem Globe Theatre auf der einen Seite, und der Revitalisierung des Nordens, mit der St. Pauls Kathedrale auf der anderen, geworden. Am Anfang war diese Brücke als ein Aussichtspunkt, von dem aus man die Stadt bewundern konnte gedacht, aber mit dem Bau der Tate Modern entwickelte sie sich zu einem der lebhaftesten Orte über der Themse.

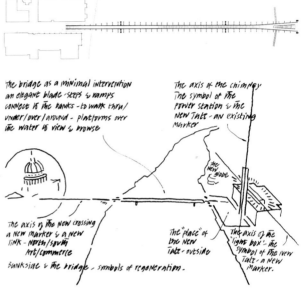

The bridge as a minimal intervention
an elegant blade - steps & ramps
connect us the banks - to walk thru/
under/over/around - platforms over
the water to view & browse

The axis of the chimney
The symbol of the
power station & the
New Tate - an existing
marker

The
New
globe

The axis of the New crossing
a New marker & a New
link - North/south
Art/commerce

The "place" of
the New
Tate - outside

The axis of the
light box - the
symbol of the New
Tate - a New
marker.

Bankside & the bridge - symbols of regeneration.

The axis produced between the city and Tate Modern materializes with the construction of this bridge. The chimney of light from the new museum connects with the city across a lighting element of aluminium and steel.

La construction de ce pont permet de matérialiser l'axe entre la ville et la Tate Modern. La cheminée de lumière du nouveau musée s'unit à la ville grâce à un élément lumineux fait d'aluminium et d'acier.

Mit dieser Brücke wurde eine Achse zwischen der Stadt und der Tate Modern geschaffen. Das neue Museum mit seiner weit sichtbaren Lichtsäule wird über dieses luminöse Element aus Aluminium und Stahl mit der Stadt verbunden.

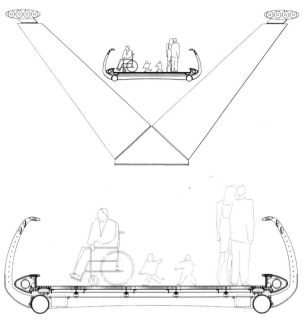

The design of the bridge's support systems was conceived to intervene as little as possible in the visual image generated from the river over the city. Thus the visual image produced is almost completely free of interferences.

Les systèmes de soutien du pont ont été conçus de manière à interférer le moins possible avec les points de vue sur la ville depuis la rivière.

Die Systeme zur Brückenhalterung wurden so gestaltet, dass diese so wenig wie möglich in die Aussicht vom Fluss über die Stadt eingreifen. So wurde erreicht, dass der Betrachtende kaum Interferenzen in seinem Blickfeld hat.

Millau Viaduct

Foster and Partners; N. Foster; K. Shuttleworth

T. Quick, A. Fehrenbach, Chapelet-Defol-Mousseigen, Agence Ter, arq.; EEG, Sogelerg et SERF, ing.

MILLAU, (AVERYON), FRANCE. 1994-2005

Length / Longueur / Gesamtlänge 2500 m.
Span / Travée / Hauptspannweite 350 m.

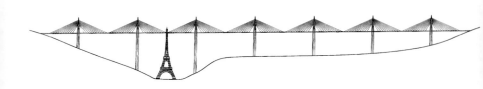

This viaduct, the winning tender design of a 1993 competition, will be built as part of the A75, the highway which will join Paris with Barcelona. One of the fundamental questions raised while projecting this passageway is the matter of carrying it out in the most economical fashion. Based on this, Foster and Partners has designed a slender line which joins the two sides of the valley with exceptional subtlety within the landscape. Even so its great structure will still be extensive: at certain points it will be higher than the Eiffel Tower and its deck will rise 275 m. above the Tarn River, a height which surpasses even that of the Commerzbank of Frankfurt, the highest building in Europe.

Ce viaduc, qui a remporté un concours en 1993, est actuellement en construction en vue de rejoindre l'A 75, route qui reliera Paris à Barcelone. Une des principales questions qui se posent au moment de ce projet est comment le rendre le plus économique possible. Tenant compte de ces facteurs, Foster and Partners ont conçu une fine ligne qui rattache les deux flancs de la vallée, subtilement introduite dans le paysage. Les dimensions de cette structure n'en sont pas moins importantes : celle-ci dépasse à certains points la hauteur totale de la Tour Eiffel, et sa plate-forme s'élève à 275 m au-dessus du Tarn, surpassant ainsi le Commerzbank de Francfort, le bâtiment le plus haut d'Europe.

Als Teil der Autobahn A 75, die Paris und Barcelona verbinden wird, wird diese Brücke, deren Baurechte bei einem Wettbewerb 1993 vergeben wurde, geschaffen. Eines der Hauptanliegen bei der Planung dieses Projekts war seine möglichst kostengünstige Durchführung. Auf dieser Basis haben Foster and Partners diese feine Linie der Verbindung zwischen den beiden Seiten eines Tals designed, die sich trotz ihrer Größe harmonisch in die Landschaft einfügt. Die Struktur nimmt beeindruckende Ausmaße an: an einigen Stellen übertrifft sie die Höhe des Eiffel-turms und ihre Plattform befindet sich an einem Punkt 275 m über dem Fluss Tarn, womit sie auch das Maß des höchsten Gebäudes Europas, der Commerzbank in Frankfurt, übertrifft.

Höfðabakkabrú and Kringlumyrar Bridges

Studio Granda
Linuhönmun, est.
Landslagsarkitekar, landscape architects Höfðabakkabrú
REYKJAVIK, ICELAND. 1995

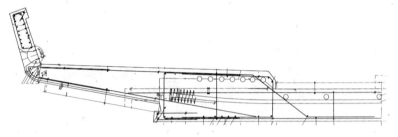

Höfðabakkabrú Bridge is part of a junction which connects a secundary road to the highway, both of which lead to Reykjavik. Its structure of prestressed concrete is composed of a deck supported by pillars. A clear and simple formal style is used to unify the structural complexity of the whole. In the same city Kringlumyrar Bridge was built as a crossing on a smaller scale to join two sections of the city which had become separated by the freeway. Thus a combined passageway for pedestrians and cyclists was projected which, owing to its appearance and actual usage has also become an urban promenade.

Le pont Höfðabakkabrú fait partie du nœud routier qui rattache une voie secondaire à la voie rapide, rejoignant toutes deux Reykjavik. Sa structure en béton précontraint comprend une plate-forme qui repose sur des piliers. Son style net et simple harmonise la complexité structurale de l'ensemble. Dans la même ville, le pont Kringlumyrar sert de connexion à moindre échelle, reliant deux quartiers de la ville jusqu'alors séparés par l'autoroute. L'image et l'utilisation de ce passage à double fonction, pour piétons et cyclistes, en font également un lieu de promenade pour les citadins.

Die Brücke Höfðabakkabrú ist Teil des Verkehrsknotens, der eine Nebenstraße mit der Autobahn verbindet, die nach Reykjavik führt. Ihre Struktur aus Spannbeton besteht aus einer Plattform, die von zwei Säulen gestützt wird. Eine klare und einfache Form und gleichzeitige Komplexität der Struktur vereinen sich bei diesem Werk. In der gleichen Stadt wird die kleinere Kringlumyrar Brücke gebaut, um zwei Teile der Stadt zu verbinden, die durch der Verlauf der Autobahn getrennt worden waren. Sie wird ein Übergang für Radfahrer und Fußgänger sein, der durch sein Erscheinungsbild und Gebrauch auch zu einem Spazierweg der Stadt wird.

.Kringlumyrar

Kringlumyrar

Höfðabakkabrú

A set of ribs within the structure of Höfðabakkabrú Bridge absorbs the vibrations produced by traffic.

La structure du pont Höfðabakkabrú comprend un groupe de nervures qui absorbent les vibrations causées par la circulation automobile.

Die Struktur der Brücke Höfðabakkabrú wurde mit Rippen versehen, die die vom Verkehr provozierten Vibrationen ausgleichen.

Höfðabakkabrú

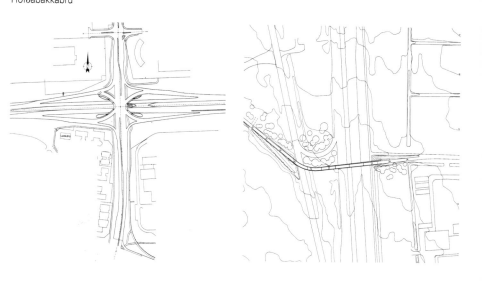

Kringlumyrar

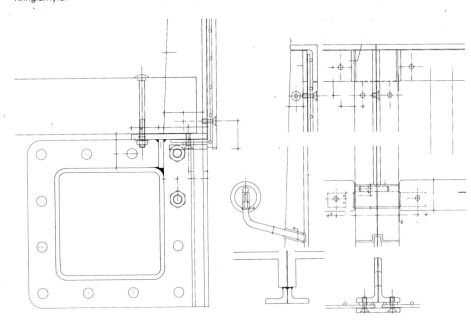

Höfðabakkabrú

Höfðabakkabrú

Höfðabakkabrú

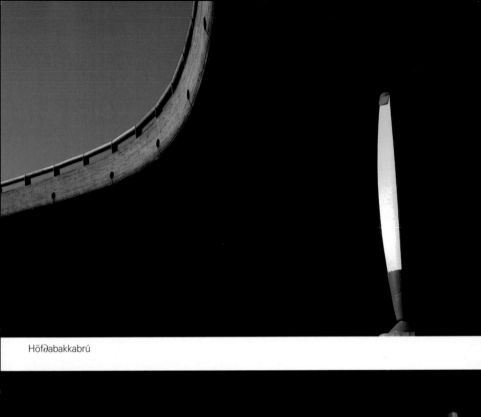

Höf∂abakkabrú

Höfðabakkabrú

Merchants Bridge

Whitby Bird & Partners

CASTLEFIELD (MANCHESTER), UNITED KINGDOM. 1995

Length / Longueur / Gesamtlänge 70 m.
Span / Travée / Hauptspannweite 38 m.

This project, winner of the competition announced by the Central Manchester Development Corporation, has become one of the symbols of the rehabilitation of the area. The dialectic existing between the field of engineering and the development of new technologies which allow the use of more geometrically elaborate shapes is resumed in the proposal of this attractive bridge. For this reason this structure is unique in the neighbourhood where, on the other hand, there exists a long-standing tradition in the field of engineering. The curve of the structure invites passers-by for a stroll on the bridge rather than merely using it as a crosswalk.

Ce projet, vainqueur d'un concours organisé par la Central Manchester Development Corporation, est devenu l'un des symboles de la réhabilitation de la zone. Ce brillant projet évoque la dialectique existante entre l'ingénierie et le développement de nouvelles technologies qui permettent de proposer des formes géométriquement plus élaborées. Cette structure est unique dans la région, où il existe par ailleurs une grande tradition dans le milieu de l'ingénierie. Le pont décrit une courbe qui invite les piétons à s'y promener plutôt qu'à l'utiliser uniquement comme chemin de passage.

Dieses Projekt, der Gewinner des Wettbewerbs der Central Manchester Development Corporation, ist zum Symbol der Rehabilitation der Gegend geworden. Im Entwurf dieser attraktiven Brücke wird die existente Dialektik zwischen dem Ingenieurwesen und der Entwicklung neuer Technologien, die die Ausarbeitung geometrisch verfeinerter Formen zulässt, zusammengefasst. So wird diese Struktur einzigartig in der Region, die über eine lange Tradition im Bereich Ingenieurwesen verfügt. Die charakteristische Kurve dieser Brücke lädt den Passanten eher zu einem Spaziergang als zu einer Wegabkürzung ein.

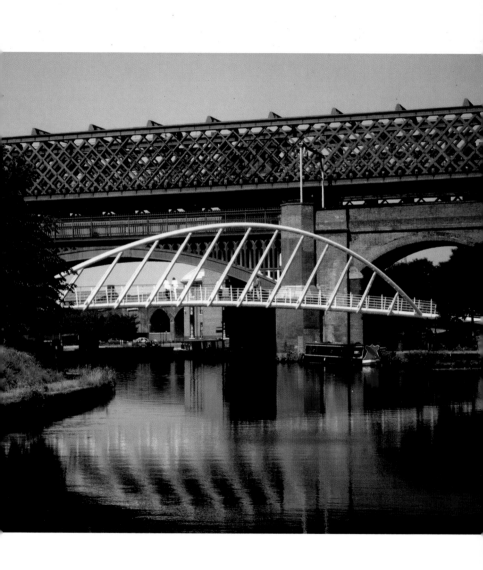

The curvature developed by the arch causes the sections of the different ribs to vary throughout the deck. For this reason as well, we can easily perceive the formal independence of the deck which functions as the connecting element.

La courbure de l'arc crée des variations dans les nervures qui longent la plate-forme de passage. On perçoit bien l'indépendance formelle de la plate-forme, qui agit comme un élément de connexion.

Die Kurve, die der Bogen entwickelt, bewirkt, dass die Größe und Form der Rippen im Laufe der gesamten Plattform etwas unterschiedlich sind. Das verstärkt den Anschein der Unabhängigkeit de Plattform als verbindendes Element.

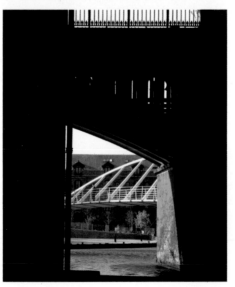

The design of the curve of the arch above the water directs our attention towards the surface, thus inviting passers-by to sway gently over the water as they stroll from shore to shore and delight in their short walk.

La courbure de l'arc se projette sur l'eau, donnant une vue sur la rivière, et incite les piétons à se balancer au-dessus de l'eau pendant qu'ils passent d'une rive à l'autre, profitant ainsi de la petite promenade.

Die Projektion der Kurve des Bogens über dem Wasser öffnet den Blick des Passanten auf dieses und lädt ihn zu einem angenehmen kurzen Spaziergang von einem Ufer zum anderen ein.

Autobahndirektion Nordbayern
Walter-Bau AG
Köhler + Seitz, est.; Max Bögl; Walter-Bau AG.

SCHNAITTACH (BAVARIA), DEUTSCHLAND.1995-1997

Length / Longueur / Gesamtlänge 1287,60 m.
Span / Travée / Hauptspannweite 105 m.

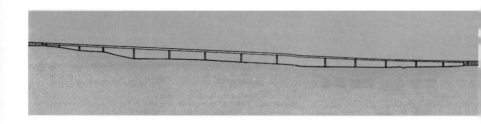

The typology of the bridges varies according to the obstacle which they are meant to overcome; thus viaducts are bridges characteristically built over dry land or in valleys and which use, in addition, a deck formed of a group of short sections. Hence Schnaittach Bridge belongs to the typology of the viaduct. This passageway forms a part of the A9 Highway with sections of differing lengths: 40,80 m, 60 m, 70 m, 90 m., 5 sections of 105 m., 4 sections of 90 m., 80 m. and a final stretch 61,80 m. long. The lengths of these sections also vary according to the orientation of the road: 1139,60 m. upwards and 1287,60 m. in the descent.

La typologie des ponts varie selon l'obstacle à franchir ; ainsi, les viaducs se caractérisent par leur construction sur des terrains secs ou des vallées, et leur plate-forme est composée d'un groupe de travées relativement courtes. Ainsi, le pont Schnaittach appartient à la typologie du viaduc. Il fait partie de la voie expresse A9 et ses travées ont différentes longueurs : 40,80 m, 60 m, 70 m, 90 m, cinq travées de 105 m, quatre de 90 m, 80 m, et la dernière de 61,80 m. Sa longueur varie également, selon l'orientation de la voie : 1139,60 m vers le haut de la colline et 1287,60 m vers le bas.

Der Konstruktionstyp der Brücken variiert je nach Art des zu überwindenden Hindernisses; Viadukte sind Brücken, die sich durch ihren Standort in trockenen Gebieten und Tälern auszeichnen und die meist eine Plattform mit mehreren kurzen Spannweiten haben. Also gehört die Schnaittach Brücke zur Gruppe der Viadukte. Sie ist Teil der Autobahn A9 und seine Abschnitte messen verschiedene Längen: 40,80m, 60m, 70m, 90m, 5 Abschnitte von 105m, 4 von 90m, 80m und ein letzter von 61,80m. Die Längen variieren in Abhängigkeit der Orientierung der Straße: 1139,60m bergauf und 1287,60m bergab.

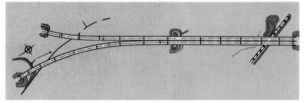

The support system of the deck is based on a series of patterned columns constructed asymmetrically throughout the length of the passage: thus the sections vary from a length of 40,80 m. at the beginning to a maximum length of 105 m.

Le système d'appuis de la plate-forme est basé sur des piliers implantés asymétriquement sur toute la longueur du passage: les travées vont de 40,80 m au départ jusqu'à 105 m pour la plus longue.

Das Stützsystem der Plattform basiert auf abgeschirmten Säulen, die asymmetrisch auf der gesamten Länge der Brücke angebracht wurden: die Länge der Spannweiten variiert von 40,80 m bis 105 m.

Pont sur la Versoix

Tremblet S.A. 1995-1998

GENÈVE–LAUSANNE, SUISSE. 1961-1962 / 1995-1998

Length / Longueur / Gesamtlänge 304 m.
Span / Travée / Hauptspannweite 56 m.

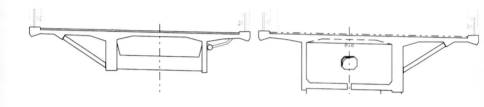

This bridge over the Versoix River, situated on the A1 Highway, consists of a pair of identical bridges of pre-stressed concrete built in 1961. This highway is normally subjected to intense traffic and although the original bridge was constantly maintained in good condition, it bacame necessary to plan an intervention on the original structure in 1995. This intervention would on the one hand take the form of maintenance and rehabilitation while on the other hand include an expansion. This was one of the most delicate requirements of the project, since it was necessary for the bridge to remain open to the public during the work while at the same time constructing an addition which would blend in with the original structure to form a single unit.

Cette construction, située sur la route A1, est formée de deux ponts identiques en béton précontraint, construits en 1961. Cette route connaît habituellement un trafic intense, et bien que le pont d'origine soit encore en bonne condition, il a été nécessaire en 1995 d'intervenir sur l'ancienne structure, d'un côté pour son entretien et sa restauration, et d'un autre côté pour réaliser un élargissement. Ceci fut l'un des problèmes les plus délicats à résoudre, car il fallait maintenir le passage ouvert au public pendant les travaux d'élaboration d'une nouvelle structure visant à former un ensemble avec le projet original.

Die Brücke über den Fluss Versoix, die sich auf der Autobahn A1 befindet, besteht aus einem Paar identischer Brücken aus Spannbeton, das 1961 erbaut wurde. Da diese Strecke immer eine besonders dicht befahrene ist und obwohl die Brücke sich noch in einem sehr guten Zustand befand, begann man 1995 mit der Planung eines Instandhaltungs– und gleichzeitig Erweiterungsprojekts der vorhandenen Struktur. Die Erweiterung war die schwierigere Aufgabe des Projekts, da die Brücke während der Bauarbeiten nicht geschlossen werden und der neue Teil eine Einheit mit dem Original bilden sollte.

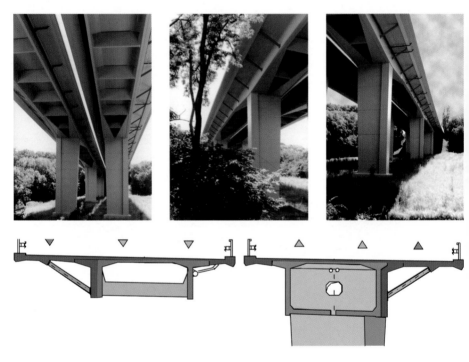

The projected expansion was developed based on the original requirements: the bridge was widened from 11 to 13,9 m. and the new deck was connected to the original to form a unit; in addition, this work was carried out maintaining two lanes open to traffic at all times.

Le projet d'élargissement évolue selon les exigences de départ : de 11 m, le pont passe à 13,9 m de large, et la nouvelle plate-forme forme un tout avec l'ancienne ; deux voies de passage sont maintenues pendant toute la durée des travaux.

Das Erweiterungsprojekt wurde auf der gleichen Grundlage wie das Original entwickelt: die Breite der Brücke wurde von 11 auf 13,9 m erhöht und die neue Plattform bildet eine Einheit mit der älteren. Während der Bauarbeiten waren stets zwei Spuren befahrbar.

Royal Victoria Dock Bridge

Lifschutz Davidson, arq.

Techniker, ing.; Equation Lighting Design;
David Langdon & Everest

LONDON, UNITED KINGDOM. 1995-1999

Length / Longueur / Gesamtlänge 157 m.
Span / Travée / Hauptspannweite 127 m.

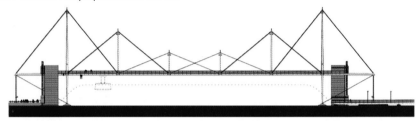

As part of the project for the reconversion of the London Docklands, an international competition was promoted in 1995. The winning proposal was that of the architect Lifschutz Davidson. A slender footbridge based on a structural design of stay cables crosses over Royal Victoria Dock. Formally, this project is a combination of metallic supports with cables which evoke the image of a ship with its masts floating over the water. The prevision of the installation of a covered deck in a lower level which would permit a protected crossing beneath the existing deck, guarantees a smoother flow of traffic.

A l'intérieur du projet de reconversion des Docklands de Londres, un concours international a lieu en 1995, remporté par la proposition de l'architecte Lifschutz Davidson, une fine passerelle piétonne basée sur le schéma structurel du pont à haubans qui traverse le Royal Victoria Dock. D'un point de vue formel, le projet réunit appuis métalliques et traverses qui évoquent l'image d'un bateau et de ses mâts flottant sur l'eau. L'installation d'une cabine est prévue dans la partie inférieure de la plate-forme pour accueillir un passage protégé au-dessus du passage existant, offrant ainsi une plus grande fluidité.

Als Teil des Projekts der Umwandlung der Londoner Docklands, wurde 1995 ein internationaler Wettbewerb zum Bau dieser Brücke durchgeführt, den das Modell des Architekten Lifschutz Davidson gewann. Ein schlanker Übergang für Fußgänger basierend auf dem strukturellen Schema der Schrägseiltechnik überquert heute das Royal Victoria Dock. Das Projekt ist eine Kombination aus Metallstützen und Stahlseilen, die das Bild eines Schiffes, das auf dem Wasser treibt, und seiner Masten vermitteln. Im unteren Teil der Plattform ist die Installation einer Kabine vorgesehen, die einen geschützten Übergang unter dem bereits existierenden ermöglicht, und so für mehr Flüssigkeit beim Überqueren sorgt.

This light and delicate metallic structure grows out of the area as if it were merely one of several boats. The height of its supports gives 15 m. of clearance to navigation beneath the deck while at the same time providing a splendid view of the area.

La structure métallique s'insère avec finesse et légèreté dans ce lieu, tel un bateau. La hauteur des appuis permet un espace libre de 15 m au-dessous de la plate-forme, qui garantit en même temps une magnifique vue du site.

Die Eleganz und Leichtigkeit der Metallstruktur vermittelt dem Passanten das Erscheinungsbild eines Schiffes. Die Höhe seiner Stützen bieten einen Freiraum von 15 m unterhalb der Plattform und garantiert außerdem eine ungehinderte Aussicht.

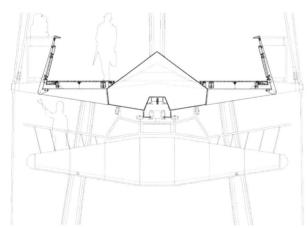

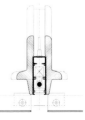

Øresund Bridge

SundLink Contractors
Skanska; Hochtief; Højgaard & Schultz; Monberg & Thorsen A/S

DENMARK–SWEDEN. 1995-2000

Length / Longueur / Gesamtlänge1092 m.
Span / Travée / Hauptspannweite 490 m.

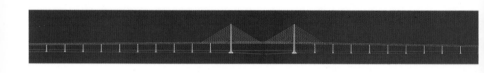

The possibility of constructing a connection between Denmark and Sweden had been studied since 1991, but it was not until 1995 that the two countries made the commitment to build this great project over the Øresund. As a linking element, this bridge built between the cities of Malmo and Copenhagen is an example of the development which can occur following the construction of a connection of these characteristics. The two cities, united by the second longest cable-stayed bridge in the world, have a total of 3 million inhabitants and function as a single unit which has become one of the 8 most important economic centres in Europe.

On étudiait la construction d'une ligne de rattachement entre le Danemark et la Suède depuis 1991, mais il fallut attendre 1995 pour que les deux pays s'engagent à construire ce grand projet sur l'Øresund. Ce pont, qui relie les villes de Malmo et de Copenhague, est un exemple du développement auquel on peut parvenir grâce à la construction d'une connexion telle que celle-ci. Les deux villes, reliées par le deuxième plus grand pont à haubans du monde, regroupent un total de 3 millions d'habitants et fonctionnent actuellement comme une même unité, qui fait désormais partie des huit centres économiques les plus importants d'Europe.

Der Bau einer Verbindungslinie zwischen Dänemark und Schweden war schon seit 1991 geplant, allerdings ergriffen die Länder erst 1995 die Initiative zur Errichtung dieses Mammutprojekts über den Øresund. Als Verknüpfungselement zwischen den Städten Malmö und Kopenhagen ist diese Brücke ein Beispiel für den wirtschaftlichen Aufschwung, den der Bau einer Brücke mit sich bringen kann. Die beiden Städte, die durch die zweitlängste Schrägseilbrücke der Welt verbunden sind, zählen gemeinsam 3 Millionen Einwohner und gehören neuerdings zu den acht wichtigsten Wirtschaftszentren Europas.

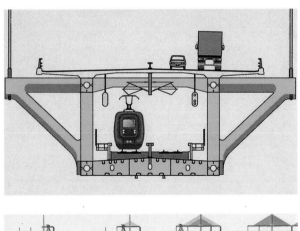

The prefabricated deck was developed on two levels: the upper level holds 4 car lanes and the lower deck, 2 railway lines which make up one of the longest decks in the world.

La plate-forme préfabriquée se développe à deux niveaux: quatre voies de voiture sont établies sur sa partie supérieure et deux voies de train sur la partie inférieure, ce qui constitue l'une des plates-formes les plus longues du monde.

Die vorgefertigte Plattform entwickelt sich auf zwei Ebenen: auf der oberen existieren 4 Fahrspuren für Autos und auf der unteren zwei Eisenbahnlinien, die zu den weltlängsten auf Brücken gehören.

In the construction of great bridges such as the Øresund Bridge, crane barges are used to transport and place the prefabricated deck sections in their corresponding positions according to the construction plan.

Pour la construction de grands ponts comme le Øresund Bridge, on utilise des bateaux grues chargés de transporter et de placer au bon endroit les pièces préfabriquées de la plate-forme selon le processus de construction.

Beim Bau von großen Brücken, wie der Øresund Bridge, benutzt man Schiffskrane, die zum Transport und zur Montage der Fertigteile der Plattform an dem für sie vorgesehenen Platz benötigt werden.

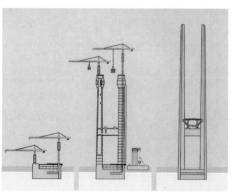

Fußgangerbrücke über Weser

Schlaich Bergermann und Partner

MINDEN, DEUTSCHLAND. 1996

Span / Travée / Hauptspannweite 105 m.

T he shores of Weser River, the location of this footbridge, boast several natural scenic landscapes: on one side we find a lovely park and on the other, a great open air area. In the background of this river we find the Porta Westfalica Monument. For this reason, when it became necessary to design a crossing over the river, the characteristics of the area suggested a design which would permit the conservation of the visual impressions of the space. Thus the decision was made to choose the suspension bridge as the model for this footbridge. The deck traces a curve which allows it to reach opposing shores which are not parallel.

L a berge de la rivière Weser, où se situe cette passerelle, fait partie d'un magnifique site naturel : d'un côté, un agréable parc, et de l'autre, un grand espace en plein air. Le monument de la Porta Westfalica s'inscrit en toile de fond de cette rivière ; quand il devient nécessaire d'établir un passage sur la rivière, le schéma le plus approprié par rapport aux caractéristiques de la zone doit être en accord avec le paysage. Par conséquent, on opte pour le modèle du pont suspendu pour cette passerelle. La courbe décrite permet à la plate-forme de rejoindre les deux rives, qui ne sont pas parallèles l'une à l'autre.

A Das Weserufer, Standort dieser Fußgängerbrücke, bietet eine interessante Naturlandschaft: auf einer Seite einen wunderschönen Park und auf der anderen einen großen naturbelassenen Raum. Den Hintergrund bildet das Monument der Porta Westfalica. Als die Notwendigkeit des Baus einer Brücke über den Fluss deutlich wurde, stand von Beginn an fest, dass die Struktur dieser die Aussicht auf die Landschaft so wenig wie möglich verändern sollte. Darum wählte man eine Hängegebrücke als Modell für den Übergang. Seine kurvige Plattform verbindet zwei nicht parallel verlaufende Ufer.

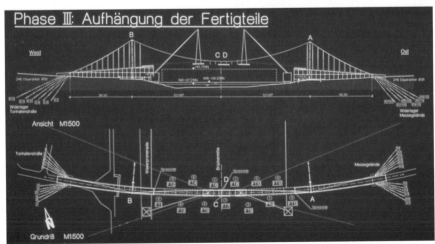

Phase Ⅲ: Aufhängung der Fertigteile

West   Ost

Ansicht M1:500

Grundriß M1:500

440

Since the two shores of the river are not parallel, the deck was designed in a curve in order for it to reach both shores uniformly. The lean of the uprights of the main structure also reflects the curvature of the deck.

Comme les deux berges de la rivière ne sont pas parallèles, on décide d'incurver la plateforme pour relier uniformément les deux rives. L'inclination des mâts de la structure principale souligne également l'incurvation de la base.

Da die Ufer der Weser nicht parallel verlaufen, beschloss man, die Plattform mit einer Kurve zu versehen. Die Neigung der Masten der Brücke steht im Einklang mit der kurvigen Form und bestärkt diese noch.

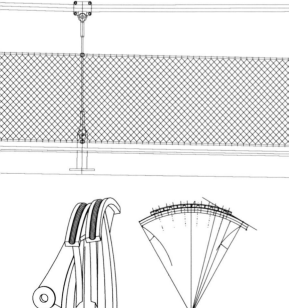

Faltbrücke Kiel-Hörn

Volkwin Marg arq.; Jörg Schlaich ing.

Architeckten von Gerkan, Marg und Partner;
Schlaich Bergermann und Partner
KIEL-HÖRN, DEUTSCHLAND. 1996-1997

Length / Longueur / Gesamtlänge 116 m.

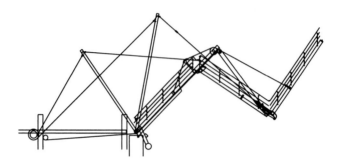

The construction of a drawbridge was promoted as part of the project for the transformation of the region near the Hörn River. The need for this bridge was clearly demonstrated by the intense industrial activity and navigation in the area. Formally, in the "closed" position the bridge presents an appearance similar to that of a cable-stayed bridge; nonetheless when it is "open", thanks to a deck which is divided into three parts, the bridge can be folded up completely. The entire articulation system depends on the lateral ball-and-socket joints operated by hydraulic motors which pull back the cables responsible for stabilizing the deck when the bridge is open for navigation.

La construction d'un pont-levis fait partie du projet de transformation de la zone proche de Hörn, primordial dans ce lieu maritime à l'activité industrielle intense. Du point de vue formel, quand ce pont est «fermé», il se présente comme un pont à haubans, et quand il est «ouvert», et grâce à la plate-forme qui se divise en trois, il peut se plier intégralement. Le système d'articulation entier repose sur des rotules latérales actionnées par des moteurs hydrauliques et qui rassemblent les tenseurs qui maintiennent la plate-forme stable quand elle se trouve en position de passage.

Als Teil des Projekts der Verwandlung der Umgebung des Hörn ergab sich die Notwendigkeit des Baus einer Faltbrücke, um der industriellen Aktivität und der aktiven Schifffahrt in dieser Gegend gerecht zu werden. Strukturell gleicht die Brücke in «geschlossener» Stellung einer Schrägseilbrücke, jedoch ist in «geöffneter» Stellung und dank der Dreiteilung ihrer Plattform ihre vollständige Faltung möglich. Ihr Öffnungssystem funktioniert über ihre seitlichen Kugelgelenken, die von hydraulischen Motoren bewegt werden und die Seile straffen, während die Brücke die Durchfahrt für Schiffe freigibt.

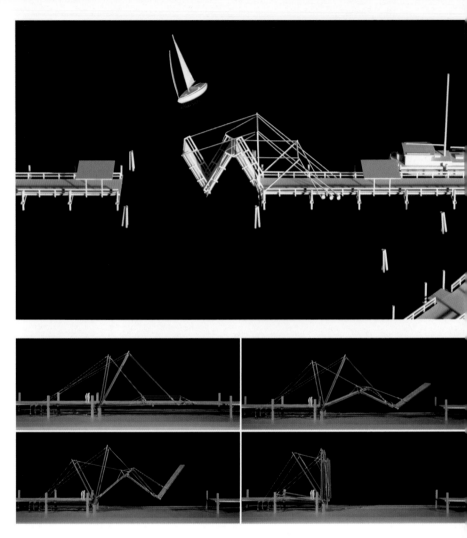

Preparing the region for the construction of houses, offices and businesses formed a part of the renovation project for the eastern shore of the Hörn River. This articulated bridge over the river was built to facilitate the connection of this new neighbourhood with the downtown area.

Le projet de rénovation de la rive est de l'Hörn prévoyait de transformer ce quartier en une zone d'habitations, de bureaux et de commerces. Pour faciliter la liaison entre cette nouvelle zone et le centre-ville, ce pont articulé a été construit sur la rivière.

Das Projekt der Neugestaltung des östlichen Ufers des Hörn sah den Bau von Wohnhäusern, Büros und Läden vor. Um eine Verbindung dieses neuen Teils mit dem Zentrum der Stadt zu gewährleisten, wurde der Bau einer Brücke beschlossen.

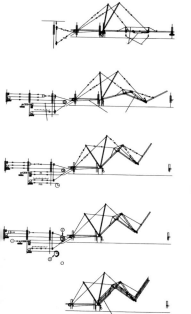

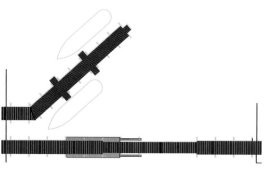

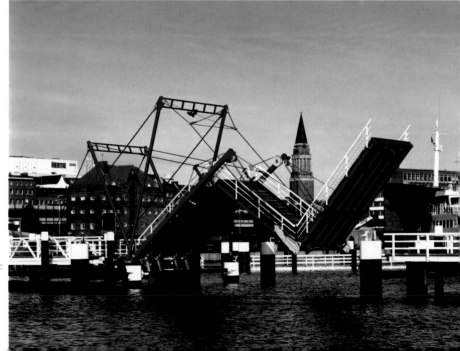

Buga-Brücke über die Elbe

PPL Planungsgruppe Professor Laage, Prof. H.G. Burkhardt
Setzpfandt + Partner GmbH Beratende Ingenieure

MAGDEBURG, DEUTSCHLAND. 1996-1998

Length / Longueur / Gesamtlänge 630 m.
Span / Travée / Hauptspannweite 250 m.

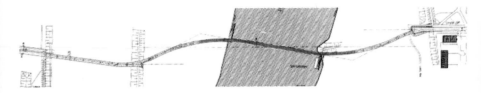

The Federal Garden Exposition was held in 1999 in Magdeburg. One of the entrances to the Exposition called for the construction of a pedestrian bridge over the Elbe River. Hence an open competition was announced for the design of this pedestrian and bicycle crossing which would also provide access to the Buga entrance of the Exposition. In this manner this suspension bridge, one of the longest in Germany, was built. Its S–shaped planimetry creates an attractive and sinuous path over the river, with views overlooking various nooks and crannies of the surrounding area. It is also possible to admire the bridge itself as one wanders down its entire length.

En 1999 se tenait l'Exposition Fédérale des Jardins à Magdeburg, et un de ses accès devait être assuré par un pont piéton sur la rivière Elbe. Un concours ouvert est alors lancé pour la conception de ce passage pour piétons et cyclistes, devant aussi servir d'entrée à l'exposition. A partir de là se construit ce pont suspendu, l'un des plus longs d'Allemagne. Sa planimétrie en forme de «S» constitue un agréable parcours sinueux sur la rivière, avec différents angles de vision sur les alentours, ainsi que sur la structure même, que l'on peut parcourir et admirer sur toute sa longueur.

Im Jahr 1999 fand in Magdeburg die Gartenbauausstellung statt und einer ihrer Zugänge musste mit Hilfe einer Fußgängerbrücke, die die Elbe überquert, gelöst werden. Also rief man zum Wettbewerb um das Design dieser Brücke auf, die Geh– und Radwege bereitstellen sollte und gleichzeitig den Buga-Eingang zur Ausstellung darstellte. Die Hängebrücke ist eine der längsten Deutschlands. Ihre «S–Form» stellt einen attraktiven kurvigen Weg her, der die Aussicht über den Fluss aus verschiedenen Blickwinkeln genießen lässt, aber auch die Möglichkeit bietet, die Brücke auch beim Überqueren in ihrer vollen Länge betrach-ten zu können.

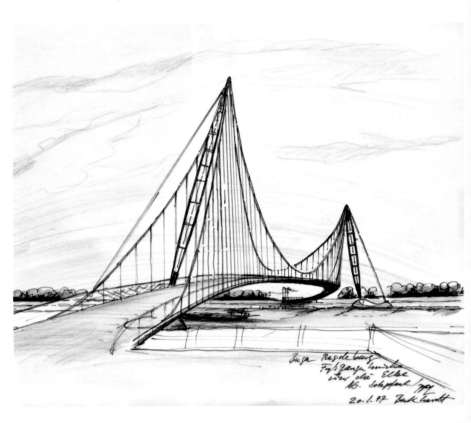

The use of a sinuous form in the planning of the deck suggests, from its planimetry, the intention of creating a path over the river. The adoption of this shape also permits one to admire the structure from any point throughout its length.

L'utilisation de formes sinueuses sur la plate-forme suggère, à partir de sa planimétrie, l'intention de créer un parcours sur la rivière. Le choix de cette forme permet également d'admirer la structure dans son intégralité.

Die Umsetzung der kurvigen Form der Plattform macht den Weg zu einem Spaziergang über den Fluss und schafft für die Passanten die Möglichkeit, beim Überqueren die gesamte Struktur der Brücke bewundern zu können.

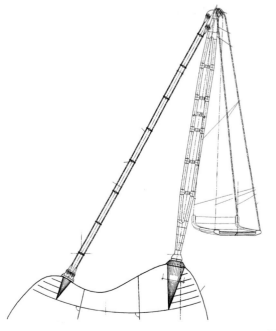

A combination of two materials was used in the structure of this suspension bridge: its metallic uprights are supported by thought-provoking concrete elements which serve as a transition to the water on both a formal and a structural level.

Deux matériaux ont été réunis pour la structure de ce pont suspendu : ses mâts métalliques s'appuient sur des pièces de béton suggestives qui servent d'élément de transition avec l'eau, tant du point de vue formel que structurel.

Beim Bau dieser Hängebrücke wurden zwei verschiedene Materialien verwendet: seine Metallmasten stützen sich auf mächtige Betonpfeiler, die formell und strukturell als Transition mit dem Wasser dienen.

Marshall Brücke

Architeckten von Gerkan, Marg und Partner. Stephan Schütz

D. Schäffler; H. Tieben; K. Beelitz

BERLIN, DEUTSCHLAND. 1996-1998

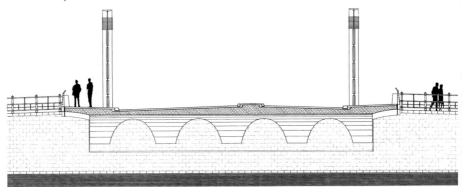

This bridge bases its structure on arches which support a deck with a combined passageway for cars and pedestrians. The approaches to the bridge are clearly identified by a pair of lighted towers at each end, which remind the users that they are about to cross a structure over water. The location of the poles of light, however, not only identifies the approaches but also indicates the different heights of the pedestrian and car lanes by rising up as a visually identifiable limit. A delicate railing on the opposite side completes the physical limits of the pedestrian path.

La structure de ce pont est constituée d'un arc qui supporte une plate-forme de passage à la fois pour voitures et piétons. Les accès au pont sont clairement indiqués par deux tours lumineuses qui signalent à l'utilisateur du pont qu'il passe au-dessus de l'eau. Les tours illuminées n'indiquent pas seulement l'accès au pont, mais elles marquent aussi la différence de niveau entre le passage piéton et la chaussée, s'érigeant en une limite visuellement identifiable. Le rôle de la fine rampe qui se trouve de l'autre côté est de compléter la limite physique du passage piéton.

Die Struktur dieser Brücke basiert auf einem Bogen, der eine Plattform hält, die den Übergang für Autos und Fußgänger ermöglicht. Die Zufahrten zur Brücke sind klar durch zwei Turmpaare markiert, von denen aus der gesamte Weg über das Wasser gut ausgeleuchtet wird. Die Lichtmasten weisen nicht nur den Weg auf die Brücke sondern dienen des weiteren dazu, die Passanten an den leichten Höhenunterschied zwischen der Straße und dem Gehweg zu erinnern. An der anderen Seite wird der Gehweg durch ein dezentes Geländer begrenzt und gesichert.

Pasarela en la Facultad de Ciencias Jurídicas

RGA Arquitectos;
Barjadí i Teixidor Associats, S.A.

B. Busom, X. Estorach, arq.; R.Brufau, est.;
M. Portell, inst.; J. Sotorres, J. Molero.

TARRAGONA, ESPAÑA. 1996-1999

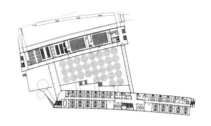

The two buildings of the Faculty of Juridic Sciences were constructed as part of the new university campus in the city of Tarragona. A central square was created between the two buildings which nonetheless became an obstacle to the functioning of the buildings as a single unit. Thus, pedestrian connections on different floors were proposed to unite the buildings in a functional manner. Of the different proposals we would like to highlight this covered footbridge which, with great formal and structural simplicity, has become the connecting element which links one building to the other at the same time that it permits the use of the central square on a lower level.

Dans la ville de Tarragone, on trouve à l'intérieur du nouveau campus universitaire les deux bâtiments de la Faculté de sciences juridiques. Ces bâtiments forment une place centrale qui toutefois constitue un obstacle au fonctionnement du complexe. Des connexions piétonnes sont alors proposées à différents niveaux pour permettre l'unification fonctionnelle de l'ensemble. Le résultat est une passerelle couverte d'une grande simplicité formelle et structurelle, qui agit comme l'élément de connexion d'un bâtiment à l'autre, et permet l'utilisation de la place centrale à un autre niveau.

In der Stadt Tarragona wurden, als Teil des neuen Universitätscampus, diese zwei Gebäude für die Fakultät der Rechtwissenschaften gebaut. Die Häuser wurden so errichtet, dass zwischen ihnen ein Platz entstanden ist, der sehr schön, aber im funktionellen Sinne auch ein zu überwindendes Hindernis für die Arbeit an der Fakultät darstellt. Also wurden mehrere Verbindungen innerhalb des Komplexes geschaffen. Wir heben hier diesen bedeckten Übergang hervor, der mit struktureller Einfachheit die Gebäude vereint und gleichzeitig die Nutzung des zentralen Platzes auf einer anderen Ebene ermöglicht.

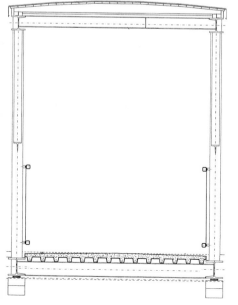

The geometry adopted for the structure permits the division of the elements into modules on both a structural and a formal level. In this manner each module is identifiable throughout the length of the passage.

La géométrie adoptée pour cette structure permet la modulation de ses éléments, tant du point de vue des formes que de la structure. De cette manière, chaque module est identifiable dans la continuité du passage.

Die übernommene Geometrie der Struktur ermöglicht die Modulation der Elemente aus struktureller und formeller Sicht. So wird jedes Modul im Laufe des Übergangs identifizierbar.

Expo 2000 Hannover

Volkwin Marg arq.; Jörg Schlaich ing.
Architeckten von Gerkan, Marg und Partner;
Schlaich Bergermann und Partner

EXPO HANNOVER, DEUTSCHLAND. 1996-2000

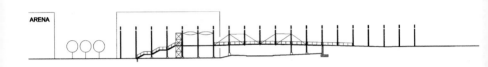

The requirements for the competition specified explicitly the need for ideas which could be used in all 4 bridge projects to be built within the exhibition site, regardless of the mode of execution. The winning bid was designed by Volkwin Marg y Jörg Schlaich. This project, with the idea of framing the entrances to be placed in the open air, proposed a forest of lighted masts lined up as "guards of honour" flanking the visitors as they wander through the exhibit. A metallic netting attached to the masts formed the structure of the passage deck of the bridges.

L'idée de ce concours était de trouver un concept pouvant être utilisé, indépendamment de son emplacement, au sein du projet de quatre ponts devant être construits à l'intérieur du parc des expositions. Le projet gagnant est conçu par Volkwin Marg et Jörg Schlaich, qui, en vue de faire ressortir les entrées situées en plein air, proposent un bosquet de mâts lumineux, alignés à la manière de «gardes d'honneur», qui accompagnent le visiteur dans son passage vers le parc. Un grillage métallique fixé aux mâts rejoint la structure de la plate-forme de passage des ponts.

Beim Wettbewerb um den Bau dieses Komplexes suchte man nach einer Idee, unabhängig von ihrer Durchführungsweise, die für alle vier innerhalb des Ausstellungsgeländes geplanten Brücken anwendbar wäre. Das Gewinnerprojekt war von Volkwin Marg und Jörg Schlaich entworfen wurden, die einen Wald beleuchteter Masten vorschlugen um die Eingänge unter freiem Himmel zu markieren. Die Masten sind so angeordnet, dass sie «Ehrenwächter» zu sein scheinen, die den Besuchern auf dem Gelände den Weg weisen. Die metallischen Netzmaschen, die an den Masten befestigt sind, wurden zu einem Teil der Struktur der Plattform der Brücke.

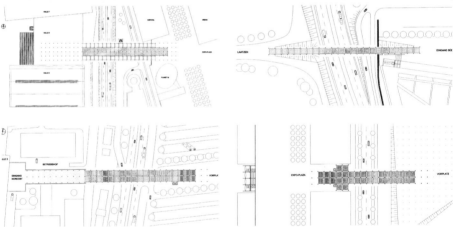

The enormous flexibility of the proposed solution allowed it to be adapted successfully to each of the 4 bridges regardless of their locations. Thus the masts become the most versatile element in the project.

La grande flexibilité de la solution proposée a permis une parfaite adaptation à chacun des quatre ponts, bien qu'ils aient été construits en différents emplacements. Les mâts constituent les éléments les plus polyvalents du projet.

Die große Flexibilität der vorgelegten Lösung erlaubte ihre korrekte Anpassung an die vier geplanten Brücken, die an verschiedenen Standorten erbaut wurden. So wurden die Masten zu den wandlungsfähigsten Elementen des gesamten Projekts.

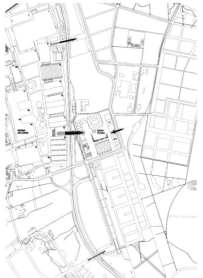

The design of the masts was of great importance: they indicate the pathway to visitors both in the form of a metallic forest as in that of a path of light. At the same time they carry the elements which support the weight of the bridge.

La conception des mâts revêt une importance particulière : ils marquent le chemin du passant, que ce soit comme bosquet métallique ou comme chemin de lumière. En outre, ils ont la fonction d'incorporer les éléments qui soutiennent la structure du pont.

Das Design der Masten ist von großer Bedeutung: der Besucher macht einen Spaziergang über einen Lichterweg durch einen metallischen Wald. Gleichzeitig dienen sie als Stützelemente für die Struktur der Brücke.

Saalebrücke Beesedau

PPL Planungsgruppe Professor Laage, Prof. H.G. Burkhardt

Schüssler-Plan Ingenieurgesellschaft mbH, Prof: Schmackpfeffer

BEESADAU, DEUTSCHLAND. 1996-2000

Length / Longueur / Gesamtlänge 805 m.
Span / Travée / Hauptspannweite 180 m.

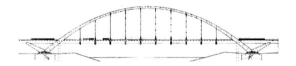

This project, which crosses the Saale Valley, forms a part of the course of the new A14 Magdeburg-Halle highway. This passage overcomes obstacles using two different methods: a raised concrete deck passing over the valley and a metal bridge over the river. Thus we also find two different types of supports: in its passage through the valley a series of short spans sustain the deck while, in order to cross the river, we find a pair of metal arches. The cables which support the "ribbing" hang from these arches in order to provide the necessary continuity to the deck.

Ce pont, qui traverse la vallée Saale, fait partie du tracé de la nouvelle voie expresse A14 Magdeburg-Halle. Tout le long de cette jonction, les obstacles sont franchis de deux manières différentes : une plate-forme élevée en béton au-dessus de la vallée, et un pont métallique sur la rivière. Nous nous trouvons ici face à deux typologies distinctes : sur le passage au-dessus de la vallée, de courtes travées se suivent pour soutenir les canaux de passage ; par ailleurs, deux arcs métalliques sont utilisés pour traverser la rivière, auxquels sont accrochés les tenseurs qui soutiennent les «côtes», donnant ainsi la continuité nécessaire à la plate-forme de passage.

Diese Brücke, die das Saaletal überquert, ist Teil der neuen Autobahn A 14 von Halle nach Magdeburg. Im Laufe dieser Verbindung werden die sich stellenden Hindernisse auf zwei verschiedene Weisen überwunden: die erste ist eine Betonplattform über dem Tal und die zweite eine Metall-brücke über dem Fluss. Dadurch finden wir auch zwei verschiedene Stütztechniken vor: über dem Tal wird die Plattform von Brückenpfeilern in kurzen Abständen getragen, während über dem Fluss zwei Metallbögen angebracht wurden, an denen die Stahlseile befestigt sind, die mit den «Rippen» verbunden sind, die wiederum die Brücke stützen.

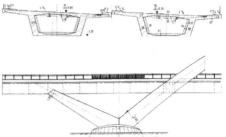

In order to continue the course of the new highway it was necessary to cross a valley and a river using the same deck. This permitted two bridge typologies to be used: the viaduct and an arched structure.

Pour pouvoir donner de la continuité au tracé de la nouvelle autoroute, il fallait réussir à regrouper le passage de la vallée et de la rivière au moyen d'une seule plate-forme. Ceci a permis de faire usage de deux typologies différentes de ponts : le viaduc et la structure en arc.

Die neue Autobahn sollte die sich in ihren Verlauf stellenden Hindernisse, die das Saaletal und die Saale darstellten, mit nur einer Plattform überwinden. Dadurch wurden zwei verschiedenen Brückentypen gebaut: ein Viadukt und eine Bogenbrücke.

The combination of two structural typologies also made possible the use of two different materials: in the valley concrete is used while the river structure is metallic. Nonetheless, the two structures constitute a single formal unit.

La combinaison de deux typologies structurales permet également l'emploi de deux matériaux différents : le béton dans la vallée, et la structure métallique au-dessus de la rivière. Malgré cela, les deux structures créent une unité formelle.

Die Kombination aus zwei verschiedenen strukturellen Typen legt auch die Nutzung zwei verschiedener Materialtypen nahe: im Tal wurde Beton und über dem Fluss Metall benutzt. Trotzdem bilden die beiden Strukturen eine formelle Einheit.

Passerelle a Leuglay

Marc Mimram, architecte
Marc Mimram Ingéniere S.A.; V. Domínguez.

LEUGLAY, FRANCE. 1997-1998

Length / Longueur / Gesamtlänge 12 m.

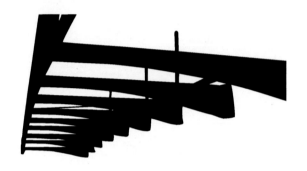

Marc Mimram architecture & ingeniere has investigated two disciplines which for them are intrinsically related. For this reason, in their professional development there exists a long tradition in the conception of bridges and footbridges which stand out for the careful architectural and constructive studies and which, above all, demonstrate sensitivity to the location. Thus this footbridge synthesizes many of the precepts of its designers. Located in natural surroundings, the footbridge includes a new component: a tree trunk which completes the structure in the form of a rafter. Thanks to this element an attractive formal structural proposal has been achieved.

L'œuvre de Marc Mimram architecture & ingénierie rassemble deux disciplines qui pour eux sont étroitement liées. Leur développement professionnel respecte la tradition dans la conception de ponts et de passerelles, qui se distinguent par une minutieuse étude architecturale, constructive et surtout sensible à l'environnement. Dès lors, se synthétisent dans cette passerelle piétonne les préceptes de ses créateurs. Située dans un environnement naturel, elle comprend désormais une nouvelle pièce : le tronc qui, tel une poutre, vient compléter la structure. Grâce à cet élément, on obtient une passerelle à la structure et aux formes attrayantes.

Die Arbeit von Marc Mimram architecture & ingeniere hat sich in zwei verschiedenen Disziplinen entwickelt, die für die Autoren untrennbar ineinander übergehen. Die professionelle Entwicklung dieser Architekten ist von der Schaffung von Brücken und Übergängen geprägt, die durch ihre sorgfältige architektonische und bautechnische Ausarbeitung und vor allem ihre Harmonie mit der jeweiligen Umgebung hervorstechen. In dieser Fußgängerbrücke vereinen sich erneut die Grundansprüche ihrer Designer an ihre Werke. Ihr Standort ist eine natürliche Landschaft, was zur Einbeziehung eines neues Elements inspirierte: ein Baumstamm, der die Struktur vollständig macht. Dank dieser Neuerung erhalten wir eine besonders attraktive strukturelle und formelle Lösung.

The limits of this footbridge are defined by two elements: an artificial one, the metal parts, and a natural one, the tree trunk. Nonetheless, its unitary conception generates an attractive dialectic between these materials.

Les limites de cette passerelle sont définies à l'aide de deux éléments : un artificiel – les pièces métalliques –, et l'autre naturel – le tronc. Sa conception unitaire engendre toutefois une dialectique fascinante entre les matériaux.

Diese Fußgängerbrücke wird von zwei Elementen begrenzt: ein künstliches –das Metallgeländer– und ein natürliches –der Baumstamm–. Zwischen beiden Materialien existiert eine interessante Dialektik, die sie vereint.

Ripshorst Brücke

Schlaich Bergermann und Partner ing.
Büro Pelle, Dortmund, ing.

OBERHAUSEN (RIPSHORST), DEUTSCHLAND.1997

Length / Longueur / Gesamtlänge 130 m.
Span / Travée / Hauptspannweite 78 m.

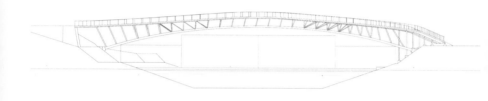

This bridge which crosses over the Rhein–Herne Canal is based on a structure made entirely of metal. The single arch is subdivided into groups of tubular pipes which serve as support to the passage deck. In addition to the curve which can be observed in the section, there also exists a curvature in the plan of the bridge as a whole. For this reason the different directions followed by various parts of the structure generate a certain visual separation of the arch from the deck: on the one hand the arch leads directly to the ground and anchors itself firmly, while the deck continues curving gently until it rests lightly upon the ground.

Ce pont, qui passe au-dessus du canal Rhin-Herne, a pour base une structure entièrement métallique. L'arc unique se subdivise en groupes de tubulaires qui servent d'appui à la plate-forme de passage. En plus de l'incurvation que l'on observe dans cette partie, une seconde est située à la base de l'ensemble, ce qui procure selon les différentes directions de la structure une certaine séparation visuelle de l'arc et de la plate-forme : d'un côté, l'arc mène directement au terrain pour s'y ancrer, et de l'autre, la plate-forme suit délicatement le cheminement de la courbe jusqu'à s'appuyer sur le sol.

Diese Brücke, die den Rhein–Herne Kanal passiert, hat eine rein metallische Struktur zur Basis. Vom Bogen gehen verschiedene Gruppen von Röhren aus, die die Plattform stützen. Zusätzlich zu der typisch kurvigen Form des Bogens macht auch die Plattform eine große Kurve und trennt sich an einigen Stellen von ihrer Base, dem Bogen, und macht sich förmlich unabhängig: an einer Uferseite wurde der Bogen direkt und auf dem kürzesten Weg im Boden verankert, während die darüberliegende Plattform eine weitere Kurve schlägt und erst danach die Erde erreicht.

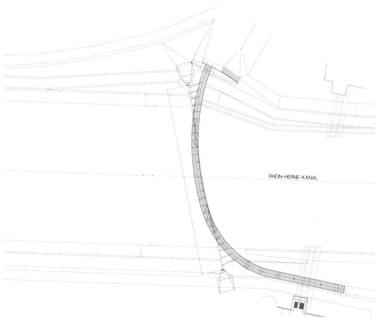

RHEIN-HERNE-KANAL

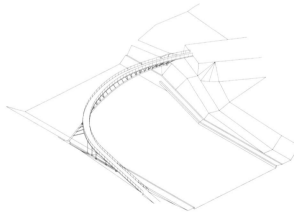

Ripshorst Bridge was conceived as a simple and unitary structure based upon the arch as support system. However, through the use of a double curvature greater dynamism is achieved in the structure.

Le pont Ripshorst a été conçu comme une structure simple et unitaire basée sur l'arc comme système de support. Grâce à une double courbe, on parvient à un plus grand dynamisme de la structure.

Die Ripshorst ist ein Entwurf, der auf einer einfachen Struktur basiert, die über einen Bogen als Stützsystem verfügt. Durch ihren kurvigen Verlauf erhält die Brücke dennoch eine spürbare Dynamik.

Passerelle Solferino

Marc Mimram, arq.

Marc Mimram Ingéniere S.A.; D. Vaniche; V. Dominguez; Sodeteg.

PARIS, FRANCE. 1997-2000

Length / Longueur / Gesamtlänge 140 m.
Span / Travée / Hauptspannweite 106 m.

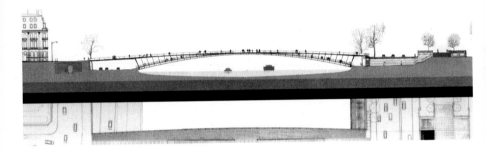

T he first Solferino Footbridge existed over the Seine River since 1859, although it was destroyed in 1961 when a provisional bridge was built. This provisional footbridge was closed off in 1992, the year in which an international competition was announced for the construction of the new footbridge. The winning bid, member of the constructive tradition of Parisian bridges, proposed an arch of a single span which would thus avoid the implantation of supports within the river. Its light and transparent structure, while providing continuity to the landscape existing on the shores of the river, would permit access from different levels to a deck connecting the two shores of the river.

L a première passerelle Solferino sur la Seine existe depuis 1859. Détruite en 1961, une passerelle provisoire est construite la même année, pour être fermée en 1992, année où a lieu un concours international pour la construction d'une nouvelle passerelle. Le projet vainqueur, conçu dans la tradition constructive des ponts parisiens, est celui d'un arc d'une seule travée, ce qui permet d'éviter les appuis sur la rivière. Prolongeant le paysage existant sur les bords de la Seine, sa structure légère et transparente permet l'accès, à différents niveaux, à une plate-forme qui rejoint les deux rives du fleuve.

S Schon seit 1859 existiert eine Fußgängerbrücke namens Solferino über die Seine. Allerdings wurde diese im Jahr 1961 zerstört und ein provisorischer Übergang erstellt, der 1992 geschlossen wurde. Im selben Jahr führte man den Wettbewerb zum Bau der neuen Brücke durch. Das Gewinnerprojekt, das dem Stil der traditionellen Pariser Brücken entspricht, besteht aus nur einem Bogen, wodurch das Anbringen von Pfeilern im Fluss vermieden wird. Als eine Verlängerung der bestehenden Flussuferlinie bietet die leichte und transparente Struktur, von zwei verschiedenen Ebenen her, Zugang zur Plattform, die beide Ufer verbindet.

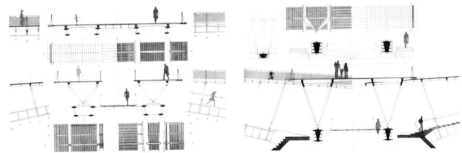

Historically the need to cross the Seine River has always existed, for this reason there exists a great tradition of bridges over this river, structurally based upon the arch. This footbridge proposes a modern interpretation of this typology.

Du besoin de traverser la Seine dans l'histoire de France est née la grande tradition de ponts sur la rivière, basés sur la structure de l'arc. A travers cette passerelle, une interprétation moderne de cette typologie est proposée.

Historisch gesehen bestand schon immer die Notwendigkeit der Überbrückung der Seine, daher auch die lange Geschichte der zahlreichen Bauten über den Fluss. Diese Fußgängerbrücke ist eine moderne Ausgabe der klassischen Version einer Pariser Brücke.

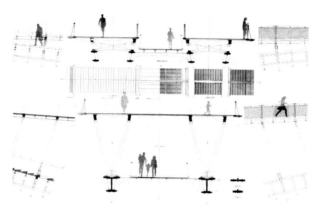

The complexity of the routes existing on the shores of the Seine
are summarized in this passageway. An asymmetrical path which
respects the different levels of the city is nonetheless introduced
within the symmetrical structure.

*La complexité des trajets existants sur les bords de la Seine peut
être observée dans cette passerelle. A l'intérieur de la structure sy-
métrique s'introduit un parcours asymétrique qui respecte les différents niveaux de la ville.*

Die Komplexität der exitierenden Wege an den Ufern der Seine wurde
in diesem Werk zusammengefasst. Innerhalb der symmetrischen
Struktur wurde ein asymmetrischer Weg geschaffen, der die
verschiedenen Ebenen der Stadt respektiert.

Gateshead Millenium Bridge

Wilkinson Eyre Architects, Gifford and Partners ing.

HARBOUR & GENERAL

GATESHEAD, UNITED KINGDOM. 1997-2001

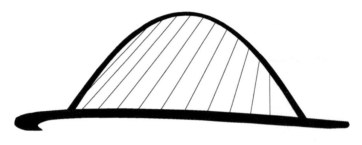

This project was the winning bid in a competition promoted by the Gateshead Council in 1997 for the construction of a new bridge over the Tyne River. A long-standing tradition of bridge-building exists upon this river, which gives it its peculiar skyline. This skyline nonetheless had not been modified for over a hundred years, but in 1999, as part of the new artistic and cultural area on the southern shore of the river, known as Gateshead Quays, construction began on the Gateshead Millenium Bridge. A slender and elegant arch forms the structural basis of a curved deck which is projected over the river as if it were a grand balcony.

Ce projet remporte en 1997 un concours organisé par le Gateshead Council pour la construction d'un nouveau pont sur le Tyne. Il existe une grande tradition de ponts sur cette rivière, ce qui lui confère son caractère de ligne d'horizon, bien qu'il soit resté plus de cent ans sans aucune modification. Mais en 1999 débute la construction du Gateshead Millenium Bridge dans le nouveau quartier artistique et culturel sur la rive sud du fleuve, Gateshead Quays. Un élégant arc filiforme constitue la base structurale d'une plate-forme courbe qui se projette sur la rivière tel un grand balcon.

Dieses Projekt gewann den Wettbewerb des Gateshead Council um den Bau der neuen Brücke über den Tyne im Jahr 1997. Der Brückenbau über diesen Fluss hat eine besonders lange Tradition und seine Skyline ist bereits durch unzählige Übergänge charakterisiert, wobei diese sich schon seit über 100 Jahren nicht mehr verändert hatte. Aber 1999 begann der Bau der Gateshead Millenium Bridge als Teil des neuen kulturellen und künstlerischen Gebiets, das als Gateshead Quays bekannt ist. Ein eleganter und schlanker Bogen ist die strukturelle Basis einer kurvigen Plattform, die sich über dem Fluss ausbreitet als wäre sie ein riesiger Balkon.

The deck is used for both pedestrian and bicycle paths, hence two levels are developed, both of which are emphasized by the use of different materials: the metallic level is for pedestrians and the perforated aluminium one for cyclists.

La plate-forme réunit le passage de piétons et de cyclistes, qui s'effectue à deux niveaux, chacun étant mis en valeur grâce au matériel utilisé : niveau métallique pour les piétons et d'aluminium perforé pour les cyclistes.

Die Plattform beherbergt einen Gehweg und einen Radweg, weshalb sie in zwei Hälften unterteilt ist, die durch die Nutzung von unterschiedlichen Baumaterialien zusätzlich voneinander abgegrenzt werden: der metallische Weg ist für Fußgänger gedacht und der aus perforiertem Aluminium für Radfahrer.

Rion-Antrion Bridge

GEFYRA S.A.
Buckland & Taylor Ltd.; Kynopraxia Gefyra; Maunsell Ltd.

PATRAS, GREECE. 1997-2004

Length / Longueur / Gesamtlänge 2252 m.
Span / Travée / Hauptspannweite 560 m.

O ne of the missions of a bridge is to surmount the obstacle presented in as short a time as possible. This is the case of the Rion-Antrion Bridge; its construction would optimize the transit situation between the ports of Patras and Igoumenitsa, in addition to facilitating communications between Greece and Italy. The characteristics of the area appeared to render the project impossible, making it difficult to take decisions on its design. Nonetheless, through an appropriate choice of technique, it was possible to turn this into one of the most ambitious projects currently underway. When completed it will be one of the longest cable-stayed bridges in the world.

L' un des rôles du pont est de franchir l'obstacle qui se trouve sur son chemin en moins de temps possible. C'est le cas du Rion-Antrion Bridge, dont la construction a optimisé les conditions de passage entre les ports de Patras et d'Igoumenitsa, en plus de faciliter la communication entre la Grèce et l'Italie. L'entreprise semblait impossible à cause des caractéristiques du lieu, ce qui a rendu la décision d'un projet difficile. Mais avec le choix d'une technique appropriée, ce projet a réussi à devenir l'un des plus grands actuellement en construction et qui fera partie des ponts à haubans les plus longs du monde.

D as Hauptanliegen der Brücke ist es, die zurückzulegende Strecke abzukürzen und so schnell wie möglich zu überwinden. Mit dem Bau der Rion-Antrion Bridge, wurde die Verbindung zwischen den Häfen von Patras und Igoumenitsa optimiert und die Kommunikation zwischen Griechenland und Italien erleichtert. Die Charakteristiken des Standortes schienen das Projekt unmöglich zu machen und machten es schwierig, sich für ein bestimmtes Design zu entscheiden. Aber durch die Wahl der korrekten Techniken ist dieses Projekt doch zu verwirklichen und so zu einem der größten sich aktuell im Bau befindlichen Projekte geworden. Die entstehende Brücke wird eine der längsten Schrägseilbrücken der Welt sein.

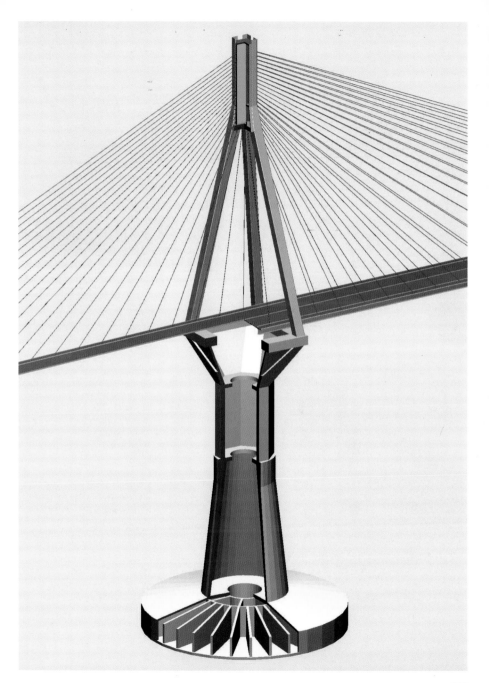

The design of each of the structural elements of this bridge will be decisive in order to overcome the adverse conditions in the area. The structure of the deck will allow it to become one of the longest ever constructed, with a continuous length of 2250 m.

La conception de chacun des éléments structurels du pont est cruciale pour pouvoir surmonter les conditions adverses du site. La structure de la plate-forme en fera l'une des plus grandes jamais construites, avec une longueur de 2250 m.

Das Design jedes einzelnen Strukturelements dieser Brücke ist entscheidend, um die ungünstigen Bedingungen des Standorts zu bezwingen. Die gewählte Struktur der Plattform erlaubt es, sie mit einer Länge von 2250 m zu einer der längsten bisher gebauten zu machen.

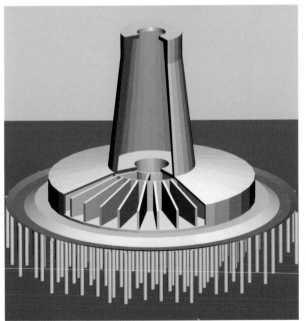

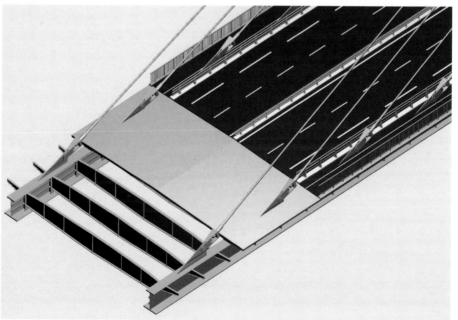

Brücke Duisburg

Schlaich Bergermann und Partner

DUISBURG, DEUTSCHLAND. 1998-1999

Length / Longueur / Gesamtlänge 77,43 m.
Span / Travée / Hauptspannweite 77,43 m.

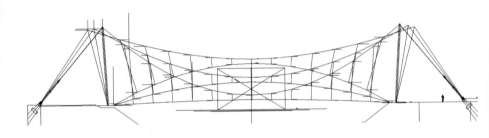

T his bridge located in the port uses the typology of the suspension bridge with posterior anchorage. An important requirement, due to the traffic in the port, was the necessity of maintaining 10,6 m. of clearance over the water level. As a result, a new drawbridge system, which would never interrupt the continuity of the passageway over the river, was projected: the main cables were designed to be capable of reducing their length occasionally and elevate thus the concrete deck. The cables are drawn back by a hydraulic cylinder, the deck lengthens and the bridge responds, providing in this manner a free passage through the water.

C e pont, qui se trouve dans un port, suit la typologie du pont suspendu avec ancrages arrières. Une des conditions essentielles de ce pont, dû au trafic important dans le port, est de maintenir un espace libre de 10,6 mètres au-dessus du niveau de l'eau. Par conséquent, on assiste à un nouveau système de pont-levis qui n'interfère pas avec la continuité du passage sur la rivière. Les tenseurs principaux ont été conçus pour éventuellement réduire leur longueur et élever ainsi la plate-forme de béton. Ceux-ci se regroupent au moyen d'un cylindre hydraulique, la plate-forme s'allonge et le pont laisse le passage libre sur l'eau.

D iese Hängebrücke, die sich im Hafen der Stadt befindet, ist an beiden Ufern verankert und hält somit die gesamte Breite des Flusses für Schiffe frei. Wegen des Schiffsverkehrs im Hafen, war es nötig eine Höhe von 10,6 m über dem Wasser frei zu halten. Aus diesem Grund, und ohne den Weg über den Fluss zu unterbrechen, wurde das neue System einer Hebebrücke entwickelt: die Spanner, die die Plattform halten, wurden so entwickelt, dass sie bei Notwendigkeit ihre Länge verkürzen und somit die Betonplattform anheben. Mit Hilfe eines hydraulischen Zylinders rollen sich die Spanner auf, die Plattform verlängert sich und die Brücke ermöglicht somit Schiffen die Durchfahrt.

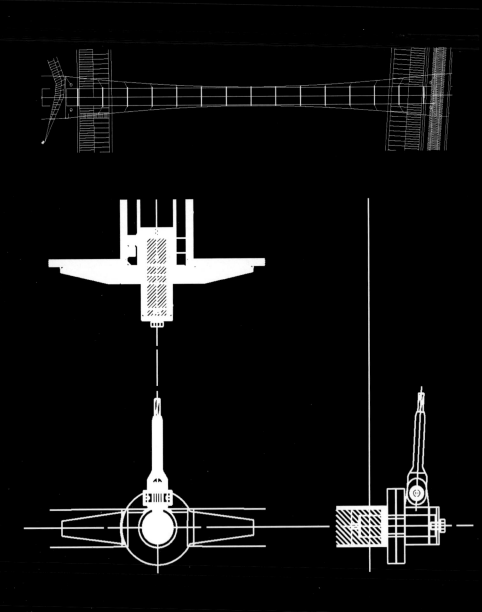

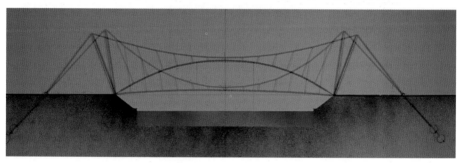

The concrete deck is a collection of sections joined by hinges which facilitate the new curvature which permits the bridge to be raised automatically. The additional length of the deck is obtained from complementary sections located at each end.

La plate-forme de béton est un ensemble de pièces unies par des charnières qui facilitent la nouvelle courbe permettant l'élévation automatique du pont. La longueur additionnelle de la plate-forme est obtenue par les pièces complémentaires situées à chaque extrémité.

Die Betonplattform ist ein Komplex aus Fertigteilen, die mit Scharnieren verbunden sind und somit die Kurve und die automatisierte Hebung der Brücke ermöglichen. Die bei der Öffnung nötige Verlängerung der Plattform wird durch Zusatzteile an den Seiten der Brücke gewährleistet.

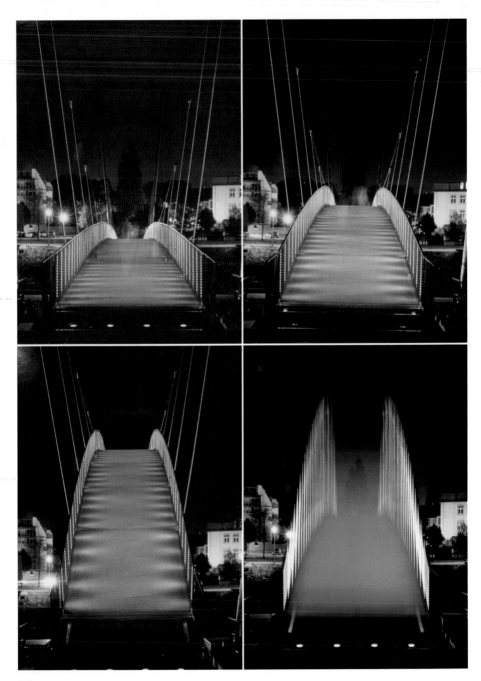

Brücke über Nesenbachtal

Schlaich Bergermann und Partner
Luz und Partner, arq.; Gertis + Fuchs, acoustics;
Prof. Reinhardt, ing.

STUTTGART, DEUTSCHLAND. 1999

Length / Longueur / Gesamtlänge 151 m.
Span / Travée / Hauptspannweite 49,5 m.

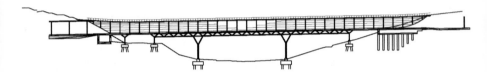

As part of the freeway between Stuttgart and Vaihingen, passing through the attractive Nesenbach Valley, we find this bridge which was designed as a protected link joining two tunnels. A metallic structure as the base sustains the concrete deck while the metallic arches give shape to the space of the main passage of the bridge. The acoustic design is of special interest: the protective barriers on both sides of the roadway and the elimination of expansion joints at the entrance to the tunnels, have succeeded in minimizing the noise including that associated with normal use such as the sounds produced by passing trucks.

Ce pont, qui traverse la magnifique vallée de Nesenbach, fait partie de l'autoroute entre Stuttgart et Vaihingen ; il constitue une ligne protégée qui relie deux tunnels entre eux. A sa base, une structure métallique soutient la plate-forme de béton et les arcs métalliques forment l'espace de passage principal du pont. Le côté acoustique a été tout particulièrement étudié: avec des barrières de protection de chaque côté des voies et l'absence de joints de dilatation au niveau des tunnels, les bruits ont été réduits au minimum, y compris les bruits habituels comme ceux produits par le passage de camions.

Als Teil der Autobahn zwischen Stuttgart und Vaihingen wurde diese geschützte Brücke über das schöne Nesenbachtal geschaffen, die zwei Tunnel verbindet. Eine Metallstruktur stützt die Betonplattform und weitere Metallbögen geben dem Hauptübergang der Brücke seine Form. Das akkustische Design wurde zu einem Hauptaugenmerk: mit geräuschblockierenden Barrieren an den Seiten und durch die Eliminierung der dehnbaren Verbindungen bei der Begegnung mit den Tunneln, wurde der Geräuschpegel auch innerhalb des Tunnels so weit wie möglich minimiert.

The metallic arches and the concrete deck give shape to the inner passageway between the two tunnels. The design of acoustic barriers as well as the elimination of expansion joints made an important control of acoustics possible.

Les arcs métalliques et la plate-forme de béton constituent l'habitacle de passage entre les deux tunnels. Le concept des barrières acoustiques et l'élimination de joints de dilatation permettent un remarquable contrôle acoustique.

Die Verbindung zwischen zwei Tunneln wird durch diese Metallbögen und eine Betonplattform gebildet. Das Anbringen von akkustischen Barrieren und die Eliminierung der dehnbaren Verbindungen ermöglichen die Kontrolle der entweichenden Geräusche.

The structure of the passage supports is completely metallic, both the main beam and the pillars form a single unit with the arches, almost as if carved out of the same metal piece, shaped and moulded until attaining a completed structure.

La structure de support du passage est entièrement métallique, et à la fois la poutre principale et les piliers forment une unité avec les arcs, comme s'ils faisaient partie d'un même élément métallique auquel on aurait donné forme afin de compléter toute la structure.

Die stützende Struktur der Plattform wurde vollkommen aus Metall gefertigt, der Hauptträger und auch die Säulen bilden eine Einheit mit den Bögen als wären sie aus dem gleichen Stück Metall gefertigt, dem nach und nach die Form der Gesamtstruktur gegeben wurde.

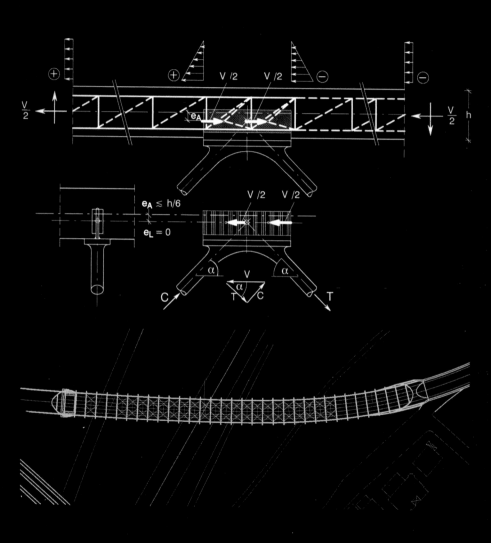

Mossops Bridge

Whitby Bird & Partners

BRIMSDOWN (ENFIELD), UNITED KINGDOM.1999

Length / Longueur / Gesamtlänge 31 m.
Span / Travée / Hauptspannweite 30 m.

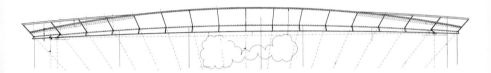

The construction of bridges or pedestrian crossings often succeeds in revitalizing areas which had become abandoned or relegated to second place for lack of a connection. This is one of the primary roles of this bridge over the Lea River. Thanks to its construction, Mossops Linear Park has been successfully transformed into one of the most important connections between the industrial area of Brimsdown and the grounds near the King George Reserve. The structure of the bridge is of metal and its deck presents a curve, both in the base and in the elevation, which confers enormous charm to the structure as a whole.

On parvient souvent, grâce à la construction de ponts ou de passages piétons, à revitaliser des zones abandonnées ou reléguées au second plan par le manque de connexion. C'est une des fonctions essentielles de ce pont sur la rivière Lea, grâce auquel on a pu transformer la Mossops Linear Park en l'une des plus importantes connexions entre la zone industrielle de Brimsdown et les terrains proches de la réserve de King George. La structure de ce pont est métallique et sa plate-forme forme une courbe qui s'élève depuis sa base, ce qui donne beaucoup de charme à l'ensemble.

Mit dem Herstellen von Verbindungen durch Brücken und Übergänge erzielt man in vielen Fällen die Wiederbelebung von Zonen, die verlassen wurden oder in den Hintergrund gerückt waren. Dies war eines der Hauptanliegen des Baus dieser Brücke über den Fluss Lea. Dank dieses Übergangs wurde der Mossops Linear Park zu einer der wichtigsten Verbindungen zwischen dem Industriegebiet Brimsdown und dem naheliegenden Gelände des King George Reservats. Die Struktur der Brücke ist metallisch und seine Plattform verfügt über eine Kurve, die dem Komplex eine besondere Schönheit verleiht.

Feichtinger Architectes
R.F.R, ing.

PARIS, FRANCE. 1999

Length / Longueur / Gesamtlänge 304 m.
Span / Travée / Hauptspannweite 190 m.

Winning proposal of a 1999 competition, this footbridge over the Seine River communicates the public square of the National Library of Paris with Bercy Park. The proposal involves a simple but elegant passage based on the play of two curving geometric shapes: the arch and the parabola. A detailed study of the possibilities of these shapes allows the passageway to be projected without any supports in the river, in addition to acquiring spatial advantages, such as the square which hangs above the river at the junction point of the two curves. The space of this square may then be used to set up temporary installations.

Ce projet situé sur la Seine remporte un concours en 1999. Ce passage simple mais élégant, qui relie la place publique de la Bibliothèque Nationale de Paris et le parc de Bercy, est basé sur le jeu de deux géométries courbes : l'arc et la caténaire. L'étude détaillée des possibilités de ces formes a permis un passage sans appuis sur la rivière qui regroupe les avantages, comme la place suspendue sur la rivière à l'intersection même des deux courbes, qui permettra le montage d'installations provisoires.

Dieses Gewinnerprojekt eines Wettbewerbs von 1999 ist eine weitere Brücke über die Seine, die den öffentlichen Platz der Nationalbibliothek Paris mit dem Bercy Park verbindet. Der Übergang ist einfach und elegant und basiert auf dem Spiel mit verschiedenen in die Struktur eingearbeiteten Kurven. Das detaillierte Studium der in Frage kommenden Formen machte es möglich, die Brücke zu befestigen ohne Pfeiler im Fluss anbringen zu müssen. Außerdem wurden räumliche Vorteile geschaffen, wie der Platz inmitten der Brücke, der an der Kreuzung der beiden Kurven entstand und eine vielseitige Nutzung ermöglicht.

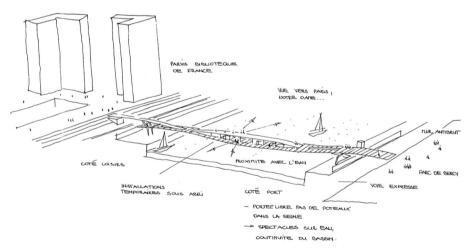

PARVIS BIBLIOTEQUE DE FRANCE

VUE VERS PARIS, NOTRE DAME...

COTÉ LOISIRS

INSTALLATIONS TEMPORAIRES SOUS ABRI

PROXIMITÉ AVEC L'EAU

COTÉ PORT

MUR ANTIBRUIT

PARC DE BERCY

VOIE EXPRESSE

- PORTÉE LIBRE PAS DE POTEAUX DANS LA SEINE

→ SPECTACLES SUR EAU, CONTINUITÉ DU BASSIN.

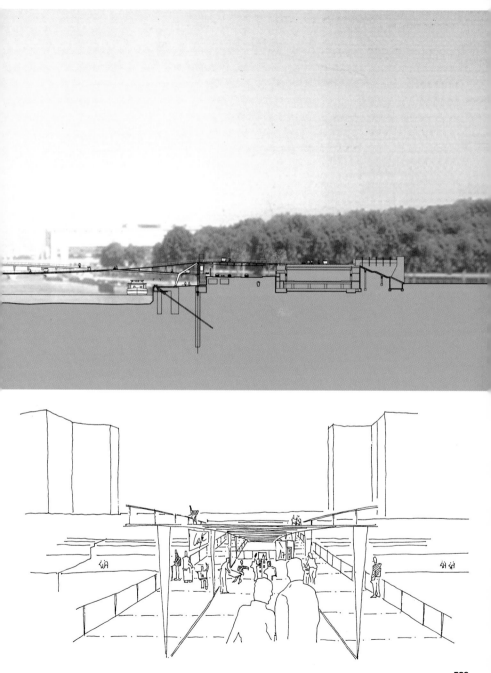

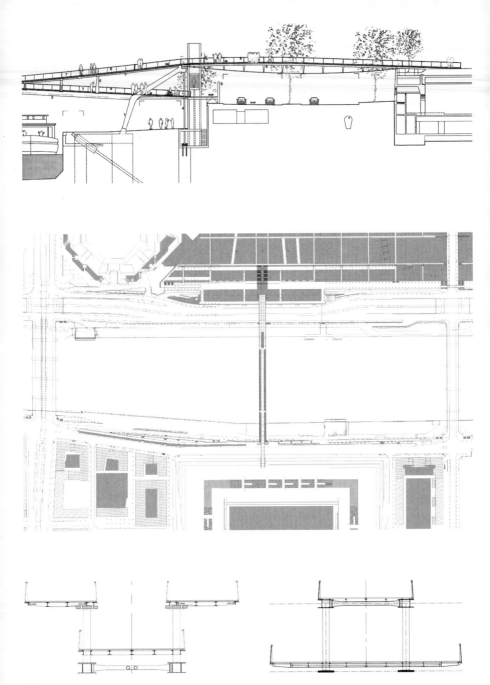

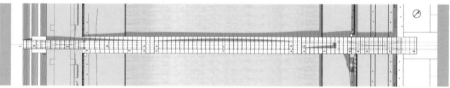

If we study the positions of some of the bridges over the river, we discover that one of the few passageways which cross the river without supports in the water is the Bercy-Tolbiac Footbridge. The virtues of the proposed geometric design have made this possible.

Si l'on observe les élévations de certains des ponts qui se trouvent sur la Seine, on remarque que l'un des rares passages qui la traversent sans appuis intérieurs est la passerelle Bercy-Tolbiac. Cela a été rendu possible grâce à la qualité de la géométrie proposée.

Beim Betrachten der Brücken über der Seine bemerken wir, dass die Bercy-Tolbiac eine der wenigen ist, die keine Befestigungselemente im Fluss benötigte. Dieser Fakt ist der raffinierten Geometrie zu verdanken, die hier zur Anwendung kam.

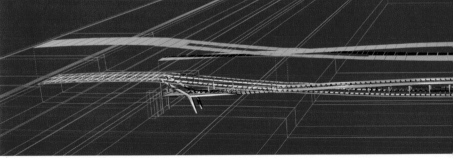

Stonecutters Bridge

Dissing+Weitling Architects
Halcrow, Flint & Neill Partnership,
Shanghai Municipal Engineering Design Institute.
HONG KONG. 1999-2000 / 2003-2007

Length / Longueur / Gesamtlänge 1614 m.
Span / Travée / Hauptspannweite 1018 m.

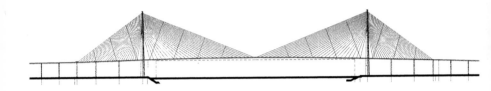

In the 1990's important connecting networks were built in Hong Kong which form a part of the actual skyline of the city today. Two more bridges will join the Kap Shui Mun, Tsing Ma and Ting Kau Bridges, promoted by the Hong Kong Highway Department: Tsin Lung Bridge and Stonecutters. The latter, winner of an international competition in the year 2000, crosses the Rambler Channel between the islands of Tsing Yi and Stonecutters. Its light and elegant structure glides into the landscape as an integral part of it: its slender pylons, great centre span and the delicacy of the design as a whole make it one of the most attractive structures designed in recent years.

Les années 1990 marquent la construction d'importants réseaux de connexion à Hong-Kong, qui font désormais partie de la ligne d'horizon de la ville. Aux ponts Kap Shui Mun, Tsing Ma et Ting Kau, promus par le Service des routes de Hong-Kong, viennent s'ajouter deux ponts supplémentaires : Tsin Lung et Stonecutters. Ce dernier, vainqueur du concours international 2000, traverse le Canal Rambler entre l'île de Tsing Yi et celle de Stonecutters. Sa structure légère et élégante se fond dans le paysage comme si elle en faisait partie : ses fines tours, sa grande travée centrale et sa conception raffinée en font l'une des structures les plus fascinantes de ces dernières années.

In den neunziger Jahren wurden in Hong Kong einige der wichtigen Verbindungsnetze gebaut, die heute Teil der Skyline der Stadt sind. Den Brücken Kap Shui Mun, Tsing Ma und el Ting Kau, die vom Hong Kong Highways Department betrieben werden, werden zwei weitere hinzugefügt: Tsin Lung und Stonecutters. Die letzte, deren Bau im Jahr 2000 durch einen Wettbewerb vergeben wurde, überquert den Kanal Rambler zwischen der Insel Tsing Yi und der Stonecutters. Ihre leichte und elegante Struktur fügt sich in die Landschaft ein, als wäre sie Teil dieser: die schlanken Türme, ihre lange Spannweite und die Feinheit des Designs des Komplexes komponieren eine der schönsten Brücken, die in den letzten Jahren entworfen wurde.

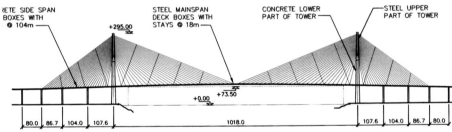

RETE SIDE SPAN
BOXES WITH
⊕ 104m

STEEL MAINSPAN
DECK BOXES WITH
STAYS ⊕ 18m

CONCRETE LOWER
PART OF TOWER

STEEL UPPER
PART OF TOWER

+295.00

+73.50
+0.00

80.0 | 86.7 | 104.0 | 107.6 | 1018.0 | 107.6 | 104.0 | 86.7 | 80.0

The elegance and simplicity of the proposed structure are the result of a study of the characteristics of the area as well as of all the visual influences surrounding the bridge and the impact of these influences upon the region, without neglecting the application of the latest technology.

L'élégance et la simplicité de cette structure sont le résultat d'une étude des caractéristiques du lieu ainsi que de tous les angles de visions depuis le pont et de leur impact sur la zone, sans oublier l'emploi d'une technologie de pointe.

Die Eleganz und Einfachheit der vorliegenden Struktur ist das Ergebnis eines intensiven Studiums der gegebenen Landschaft, des Impakts der Brücke in ihr und der Analyse aller verschiedener Ansichten des Gebaus, wobei technologische Gesichtspunkte nie außer Acht gelassen wurden.

Due to their slender and willowy proportions, the elegant concrete and metal pylons will form a part of the skyline as if they were merely one more of several skyscrapers. With their tremendous height of a total of 290 m., however, they create a unified image with the rest of the structure.

Les élégantes tours de béton et métal, aux formes étroites et allongées, forment la ligne d'horizon à la manière d'un gratte-ciel. D'une hauteur de 290 m au total, elles constituent cependant une unité avec le reste de la structure.

Durch die schmalen und langen Proportionen der Brücke werden sich die eleganten Masten aus Beton und Metall in die Skyline einfügen, als wären sie Wolkenkratzer. Trotz ihrer enormen Höhe von 290 m formen sie ein einheitliches Bild mit dem Rest der Struktur.

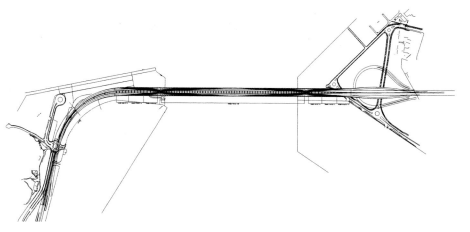

Pont sur La Meuse a Chooz

Marc Mimram, arq.
Marc Mimram Ingéniere S.A.; J.L. Calligaro; L. Becker.

ARDENNES, FRANCE. 2000-2002

Length / Longueur / Gesamtlänge 112 m.
Span / Travée / Hauptspannweite 52 m.

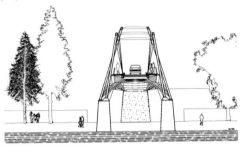

In the wooded region of Ardennes, situated in the centre of the Paris-Brussels-Cologne triangle, we find the town of Chooz where this project, commissioned by the Commune of this city, is located. This bridge emerges out from the tree-lined shores of the Meuse River and crosses it. Four piers in the water bear the weight of the metal arches which sustain the deck. With a total span of 112 m., the deck is divided into three sections measuring 30 m., 52 m. and 30 m. The arches, which cover the centre span, "rebound" as they come in contact with the piers in order to reach the shores thus completing the structure of the bridge.

Dans la région boisée des Ardennes, on trouve au centre du triangle Paris/Bruxelles/Cologne la ville de Chooz, site de ce projet pris en charge par la Commune de la ville. Ce pont s'élève au-dessus de la Meuse, depuis les rives bordées d'arbres. Quatre piliers sur l'eau reçoivent le groupe d'arcs métalliques qui soutient la plate-forme. D'une longueur totale de 112 m, les travées se séparent en trois parties de 30, 52 et 30 m. Les arcs, qui recouvrent la travée centrale, «rebondissent» au point de rencontre avec les piliers pour rejoindre les rives et compléter la structure.

In der waldreichen Gegend der Ardennen, im Zentrum des Dreiecks Paris, Brüssel und Köln, befindet sich der Ort Chooz, wo dieses Projekt von der Commune der Stadt in Auftrag gegeben wurde. Diese Beücke entspringt dem von Bäumen Gesäumten Ufer des Flusses Meuse und überquert ihn. Vier Säulen im Wasser stützen die Gruppen von Metallbögen, die die Plattform tragen. Die Gesamtlänge von 112 m unterteilt sich in drei Abschnitte von 30, 52 und nochmal 30 m. Die Bögen, die der Länge der Hauptspannweite entsprechen, scheinen beim Kontakt mit den Säulen «abzuprallen», um dann zu den Ufern zu gelangen und die Struktur zu vervollständigen.

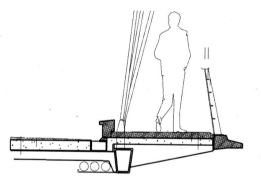

With the arch as the basic structural element, two pairs are proposed which, united by ribs, together form a single formal unit. Upon arriving at the supports, two additional arches stretch out to sustain the deck from below in order to complete the structure.

Utilisant l'arc comme élément de base, ce pont en comporte deux paires qui, unies aux nervures, se transforment en une unité formelle. Pour compléter la structure, deux arcs supplémentaires partent des appuis et soutiennent la plate-forme par le bas.

Statt der üblichen zwei Bögen wurden hier zwei Bogenpaare vorgeschlagen, die untereinander durch Rippen verbunden sind und so zu einer Einheit werden. Beim Auftreffen dieser auf die Säulen, gehen von dort zwei weitere Bogenpaare ab, um die Struktur unterhalb zu stabilisieren.

28 m

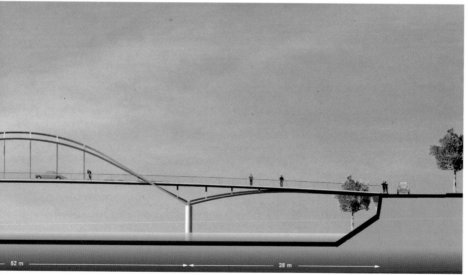

The two pedestrian walkways are separated from the car lanes by a barrier formed by the very structure of the bridge: the group of supporting cables which run from the arch to the deck. Looking out towards the river, a metal railing protects the stroller as he admires the landscape.

Les deux passages piétons sont séparés de la chaussée par une barrière qui émerge de la structure elle-même : le groupe de tenseurs qui va de l'arc à la plate-forme. Une rampe métallique, qui suit le chemin jusqu'à la rivière, protège le passant alors qu'il admire le paysage.

Die zwei Gehwege sind von der Fahrbahn durch eine Barriere abgetrennt, die aus der eigenen Struktur der Brücke hervorgeht: die Spanner, die vom Bogen zur Plattform gelangen. Der Passant wird durch ein Metallgeländer beim Überqueren geschützt.

Ribble Way Footbridge

Wilkinson Eyre arq.;
Flint & Neill Partnership ing.

LANCASHIRE, UNITED KINGDOM. 2000-2002
Span / Travée / Hauptspannweite 43,5 m.

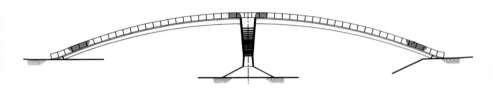

T he connection known as Hacking Ferry which forms a part of Ribble Road has existed since the 14th century. When the ferry went out of service in the mid-1950's, this connection became a complicated and dangerous crossing. A competition promoted by the Lancashire County Council proposed the restoration of the original route while at the same time including it as part of a larger scale network. In this manner, the proposal for this attractive passageway consisting of three roads over the Ribble and Calder Rivers was born. On account of its construction, the decision was made to build the entire structure elsewhere and transport it afterwards, in a single piece, by means of a helicopter.

L a connexion Hacking Ferry, qui fait partie du chemin de Ribble, existe depuis le 14ème siècle. Au milieu des années cinquante, lorsque le ferry cesse de fonctionner, cet élément de rattachement devient un passage compliqué et dangereux. Un concours promu par le Lancashire County Council propose de restaurer la route d'origine, et de l'inclure dans un réseau à plus grande échelle. C'est ainsi que le projet de ce somptueux pont, formé de trois voies sur les rivières Ribble et Calder, voit le jour. Pour son implantation, on décide de construire la structure entière à l'extérieur et de la transporter ensuite, en une seule pièce, à l'aide d'un hélicoptère.

B ereits seit dem 14. Jahrhundert existierte eine Verbindung, die als Hacking Ferry bekannt war und Teil des Ribble Way bildete. Mitte der 50er Jahre, als die Fähre schon nicht mehr funktionierte, wurde diese Verbindung zu einem komplizierten und gefährlichen Übergang. Beim Wettbewerb um den Bau einer neuen Brücke, der vom Lancashire County Council veranstaltet wurde, suchte man nach einer Lösung, die die Originalroute erhält und diese gleichzeitig erweitert. So kam es zu dieser attraktiven dreiwegigen Brücke über die Flüsse Ribble und Caldar. Das Problem ihrer schwierigen Installation löste man, indem man die gesamte Struktur fern ihres späteren Standortes anfertigte und sie dann mit Hilfe eines Hubschraubers in einem Stück zum Fluss transportierte.

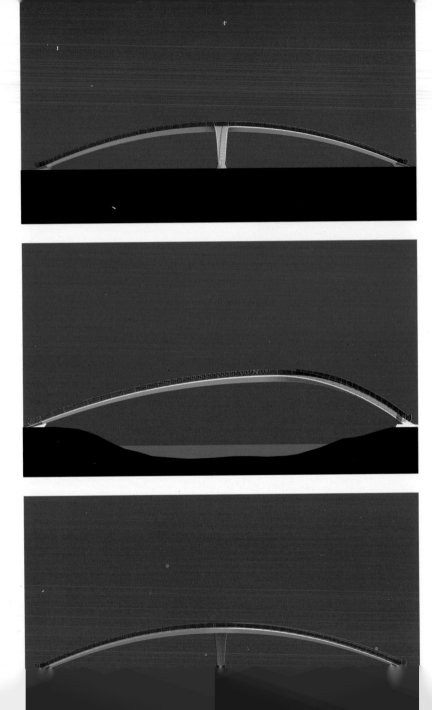

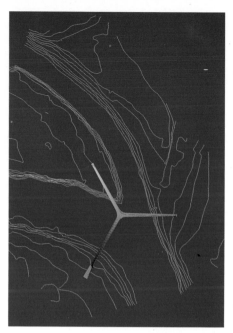

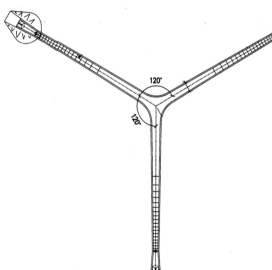

In order to cross both rivers a single structure was proposed, which would nonetheless follow the three different directions of the shores. Thus a set of arches with spans of equal lengths replaces what was originally meant to be two bridges.

Pour traverser les deux rivières, on propose une seule structure, mais qui suit les trois directions des rives. Ainsi, un ensemble d'arcs de travées égales se substitue à ce qui devait être à l'origine deux ponts distincts.

Um die beiden Flüsse zu überqueren schlug man eine einzige Struktur vor, die alle drei Ufer erreichen und miteinander verbinden sollte. Ein Bögenkomplex mit drei gleichen Spannweiten übernimmt also die Funktion, die ursprünglich zwei Brücken hatten.

Wilkinson Eyre arq.;
Flint & Neill Partnership ing.
Balfour Beatty Construction Limited

CORNWALL, UNITED KINGDOM. 2001

Length / Longueur / Gesamtlänge 47,9 m.
Span / Travée / Hauptspannweite 47 m.

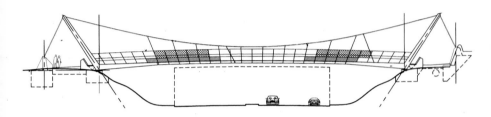

The Cornish Route, part of the UK National Cycle network, passes over the A30 Highway and comes to an end in the region of Cornwall. Its use is not restricted to pedestrians, cyclists and horse-riders may also cross upon it. This project was the winner of a competition in which a design of great technical quality, which would also be economical and easy to maintain, was demanded. The great innovation of this passageway lies in its use of new materials for the structure: the prefabricated fibreglass deck with reinforced plastic (GRF) is the basis of the passageway. From the A30 Highway we can see a floating platform rising out of a dense tree-filled area.

La route Cornish, qui appartient au réseau UK National Cycle, passe au-dessus de la voie rapide A30, complétant ainsi le trajet vers la zone de Cornouailles. Cette passerelle n'est pas seulement réservée aux piétons : cyclistes et personnes à cheval peuvent également traverser. Ce projet a remporté un concours qui exigeait la conception d'un pont d'une grande qualité au point de vue technique, économique et facile à entretenir. La grande innovation de ce passage réside dans l'utilisation de nouveaux matériaux pour sa structure : une plate-forme préfabriquée en fibre de verre avec plastique renforcé (GRF) constitue la base du pont. On peut apercevoir depuis l'A30 sa plate-forme flottante émerger d'un bois dense.

Die Cornish Route, Teil des UK National Cycle Netzes, führt auch über die Autobahn A30 und vervollständigt dort den Teil ihrer Strecke, der durch Cornwall verläuft. Die Brücke wird nicht nur von Fußgängern, sondern auch von Radfahrern und Reitern benutzt. Dieser Entwurf gewann den Wettbewerb, bei dem eine Brücke in Auftrag gegeben wurde, deren Instandhaltung unkompliziert und Kosten gering wären, wobei sie natürlich auch die gewünschte technische Qualität haben sollte. Die Innovation bei diesem Übergang liegt in der Verwendung neuer Materialien: die vorgefertigte Plattform besteht aus Glasfaserplatten und verstärktem Plastik (GRF). Von der A30 aus sieht man eine schwebende Plattform, die aus einem dichten Waldstück hervorgeht.

565

50x50x6 Pultruded GRP
angle cleat bonded to
edge beam and deck   100

Recycled rubber block
equestrian surface

40

GRP sandwich
deck panel

GRP edge beam,
thickness varies
8.9-12.6mm   100

250

Hand laid boundary
angle 100x100x6mm

70x5 S/S strip
bolted through GRP   100

GRP bottom skin
sandwich panel

GRP transverse web

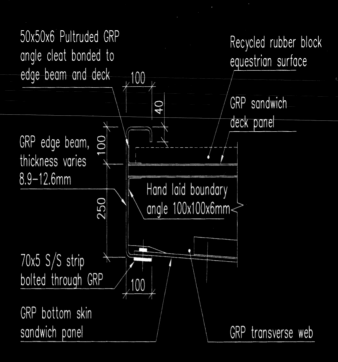

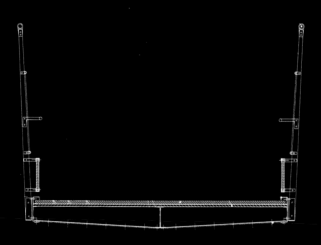

The area at both ends of the crosswalk is completely covered with trees so that the pylons of the structure remain almost entirely concealed from the fleeting view of passers-by on the highway. On the other hand, the pedestrians are able to perceive the delicate structure in its entirety.

Des arbres bordent le passage de chaque côté. De cette manière, les tours de la structure sont pratiquement cachées à la vision fugitive depuis l'autoroute. Au contraire, les piétons peuvent observer la délicate structure dans son intégralité.

Beide Seiten des Übergangs sind von Bäumen umgeben, wodurch die Masten der Brücke fast vollständig versteckt sind und sie dem Passanten der Autobahn kaum sichtbar werden. Im Gegensatz dazu kann der Fußgänger die gesamte feine Struktur wahrnehmen.

Hungerford Bridge

Lifschutz Davidson, arq.
WSP Group; David Langdon & Everest
LONDON, UNITED KINGDOM. 2001

Length / Longueur / Gesamtlänge 320 m.

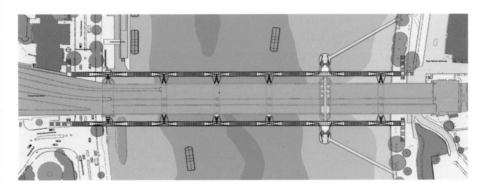

T his passageway is one of the Millenium Projects which were developed in the city of London and which achieved the construction of diverse projects such as Tate Modern and the Jubilee Line of the London subway. For this competition, organized by the Westminster City Council in 1996, an important pre-existing element used was the Charing Cross Railway Bridge, which would be the starting point for the new passages to be designed. Thus, a pair of pedestrian bridges would be the connecting element between the West End and the southern shore, acquiring in this manner, the status of one of the most important interventions to be carried out in this area.

C e passage est l'un des Millenium Projects développés à Londres et qui ont engendré les constructions de projets divers tels que la Tate Modern ou la Jubilee Line du métro londonien. Ce concours, organisé par le Westminster City Council en 1996, constituait à concevoir de nouveaux passages sur l'important pont ferroviaire déjà existant de Charing Cross. Deux ponts piétonniers formeront le point de connexion entre la West End et la rive sud ; ce sera l'une des plus importantes interventions réalisées dans le quartier.

D ieser Übergang ist Teil der Millenium Projects, die in London entwickelt werden und so diverse Projekte wie die Tate Modern und die Jubilee Line der Londoner Metro einschließen. Bei diesem 1996 vom Westminster City Council organisierten Wettbewerb stand die Eisenbahnbrücke Charing Cross als Ausgangsbasis zur Verfügung, von der aus man die neuen Übergänge entwarf. Hier werden zwei Fußgängerbrücken als Verbindungspunkt zwischen dem West End und dem Südufer entstehen, die in diesem Gebiet gleichzeitig eine der bedeutendsten architektonischen Veränderungen darstellen.

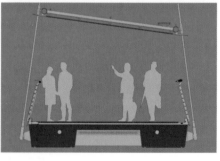

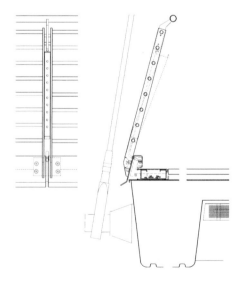

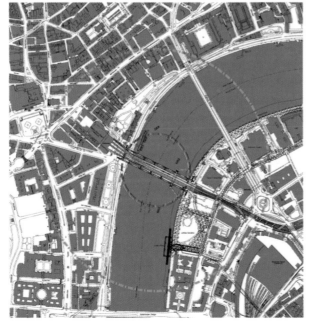

The new pedestrian link across the river consists of two lanes flanking the already existing railway bridge. It would be one of the most important connections joining the cultural and leisure area with Trafalgar Square and the West End.

La nouvelle liaison piétonne sur la rivière est divisée en deux passages qui entourent la voie ferrée déjà existante. Elle représentera l'une des plus importantes connexions reliant le quartier culturel et de loisirs avec Trafalgar Square et la West End.

Die neue Fußgängerbrücke über den Fluß besteht aus zwei Bahnen, die seitlich der bereits bestehenden Eisenbahnbrücke verlaufen. Sie wird damit zu einer der wichtigsten Verbindungen zwischen dem Kultur- und Freizeitbereich der Stadt und dem Trafalgar Square und West End.

Photography Credits • Crédits photographiques • Fotografen

©Fernando Alda / Archivo fotográfico de Expo 92 (*Puente La Barqueta*)

©Paco Asensio (*Ponte Vasco da Gama*)

©Mandy Bates (*Hungerford Bridge*)

©Schlaich Bergermann und Partner (*Ripshorst Brücke, Ting Kau, Fubgangerbrücke über Neckar, Brücke über Nesenbachtal, Brücke Duisburg, Fubgangerbrücke über Weser, Humboldthafen Brücke*)

©Jordi Bernadó (*Pasarela sobre el Segre de los arq. Mamen Domingo, Ernest Ferré*)

©Whitby Bird & Partners (*Thames Court Footbridge, Mossops Bridge*)

©Max Bögl Bauunternehmung GmbH & Co. KG (*Talbrücke Schnaittach*)

©Robert Brufau (*Puente peatonal sobre el río Segre*)

©Buckland & Taylor (*Alex Fraser Bridge, Lions Gate Bridge*)

©Lluís Cantallops (*Pasarela Estanque de la Cobertera*)

©Lluís Casals (*Pasarela en la Avda. Meridiana; Pasarela junto a plaza Karl Marx*)

©Peter Cook / VIEW (*Merchants Bridge*)

©Hayes Davidson / Nick Wood (*Hungerford Bridge*)

©Lifschutz Davidson (*Royal Victoria Dock Bridge, Hungerford Bridge*)

©DSD Dillinger Stahlbau GmbH (*Ponte 25 de Abril, Pont de Normandie, Brücke Suderelbe, Rheinbrücke Speyer*)

©Daylight S.P.R.L (*Wandre Bridge*)

©Feichtinger Architectes (*Passerelle Bercy-Tolbiac*)

©Figg Engineering Group (*Natchez Trace Parkaway Arches*)

©Flint & Neill Partership (*Stonecutters Bridge, Ribble Way Footbridge, Halgavor Foobridge*)

©Gérard Forquet (*Pont Bourgogne, Pont Antrenas*)

©Foster and Partners (*Millau Viaduct, Millenium Bridge*)

©Foto Fuchs, Magdeburg (*Buga-Brücke über die Elbe*)

©Foto Schüler, Zella-Muhlis (*Saalebrücke Beesadau*)

©Klaus Frahm (*Expo Hannover, Faltbrücke Kiel-Hörn*)

©Freyssinet (*Ponte Vasco da Gama, Pont de Normandie*)

©Gefyra (*Rion-Antrion*)

©Dennis Gilbert / VIEW (*Millenium Bridge*)

©Gleitbau Salzburg (*Helgeland Bridge*)

©Nick Guttridge / VIEW (*Gateshead Millenium Bridge*)

©Halcrow Group LTD (*Second Severn Crossing, Stonecutters Bridge*)

©Highways Department. Hong Kong (*Kap Shui Mun, Tsing Ma, Ting Kau*)

©Hiroshima Prefecture (*Akinada, Kaita*)

©Hochtief (*Great Belt Bridge, Bosporus Bridge*)

©Bart Hofmeester/Aerocamara (*Van Brienenoord Bridge*)

©Honshu-Shikoku Bridge Authority (*Kojima Sakaide Route, Kobe Naruto Route, Onomichi Imabari Route*)

©Jean Françoise Klein (*Pont sur la Versoix*)

©David Lee (*Humber River Bridge*)

©Heiner Leiska (*Faltbrücke Kiel-Hörn*)

©Mott MacDonald (*Tsing Ma*)

©Duccio Malagamba (*Pasarela Petrer*)

©Pierre Mens (*Øresund Bridge*)

©Marc Mimram (*Passerelle Solférino, Passerelle a Leuglay, Pont sur la meuse a Chooz*)

©Jordi Miralles (*Pasarela Urbitarte*)

©Monberg & Thorsen A/S (*The Faro Bridges, Pont de Normandie, Askoy Bridge, New Little Belt Bridge, Great Belt East Bridge, Øresund Bridge*)

©Jaap Oepkes (*Mossops Bridge*)

©Parsons (*Williamsburg Bridge, Great Belt Bridge, Ponte 25 de Abril, Carquinez Strait Bridge, Tacoma & New Tacoma Narrows Bridge, Woodrow Wilson Bridge*)

©PPL Hamburg (*Neue Werrabrücke*)

©rga Arquitectes (*Pasarela en la Facultad de Ciencias Jurídicas*)

©Marcus Robinson (*Royal Victoria Dock Bridge*)

©Emilio Rodríguez Ferrer (*Puente de Bac de Roda, Felipe II*)

©Gleitbau Salzburg (*Tsing Ma*)

©Jürgen Schmidt (*Expo Hannover*)

©Sigurgeir Sigurjónsson (*Höfdabakkabrú y Kringlumyrar Bridge*)

©Sill (*Marshall Brücke*)

©Grant Smith / VIEW (*Millenium Bridge*)

©María J. Sörensen (*Van Brienenoord Bridge*)

©Stretto di Messina S.P.A (*Il ponte sullo Stretto di Messina*)

©Hisao Suzuki (*Puente industrial «Camy-Nestle»*)

©Techniker (*Royal Victoria Dock Bridge*)

©Frances Tur (*Sancho el Mayor*)

©Hans Werlemann (*Footbridge in Museumpark*)

©X-M (*Estación Lehrter*)

This book was made possible thanks to the collaboration of the people who have been directly and indirectly related to this project and, above all, to the architectural and engineering firms who have provided us with the material. We wish to extend our gratitude to all of them for their collaboration and most especially to:

Cet ouvrage a été possible grâce à la collaboration des personnes liées directement ou non à ce projet, et surtout aux bureaux d'architecture et d'ingénierie qui ont mis leur matériel à notre disposition, que nous tenons à remercier pour leur collaboration. Nous remercions tout particulièrement :

Dieses Buch wurde dank der Mitarbeit aller der Personen möglich, die sich direkt oder indirekt an diesem Projekt beteiligt haben, vor allem aber durch die Unterstützung der Architektur- und Ingenieurbüros, die uns das notwendige Material zur Verfügung gestellt haben. Darum gilt unser besonderer Dank:

Bettina Ahrens (GMP)
Ariadna Àlvarez Garreta
Pedro Barboza
Barbara Berg (Gleitbau Salzburg)
Robert Brufau
Roger Buckby, Caroline Tong
 (Halcrow Group LTD.)
Lluis Cantallops
Laure Celeste (Freyssinet)
Andres Canakis
KT Cheung (Highways Department. Hong Kong)
Lifschutz Davidson
Vicente Domínguez (Marc Mimram)
Mamen Domingo, Ernest Ferre
R. A. Evans (Humber River Board)
Ramón Farré-Escofet i Paris
Barbara Feichtinger (Feichtinger Architectes)
Ian Firth (Flint & Neill Partnership)
Mireia Fornells (Enric Miralles & Benedetta
 Tagliabue arquitectes associats)
Imke Frühling (PPL Planungsgruppe
 Professor Laage)
Gladys Galer (Parsons)

Gefyra
Katy Harris, Elizabeth Walker
 (Foster and Partners)
Hiroshima Prefectural Government Officce
Toyoaki Ito (Honshu-Shikoku Bridge Authority)
Jocelyne Jacob (SETRA)
Nicolas Jangberg (Köhler + Seitz)
Julia Johnson (Whitby Bird & Partners)
Jean Françoise Klein (Tremblet S.A.)
Guido Krumbach (Hochtief)
Inge Lise Leihof (Monberg & Thorsen A/S)
Cheryl Loukas (Buckland & Taylor)
Mott MacDonald
Cheryl Maze (Figg Engineering Group)
Merce Natividad (rga arquitectes)
OMA
Carme Pinos, Flora
Beatriz Quintanero (DSD)
Beatriz Salvatierra
Gigli Sandro (Stretto di Messina S.P.A)
Jörg Schlaich (Schlaich Bergermann
 und Partner)
Alfons Soldevila